If I
Were In
My Thirties

If I Were In My Thirties

by

Rufus Jones

THOMAS NELSON INC., PUBLISHERS

Nashville   •   New York

The Scripture quotations in this publication are from the Revised
Standard Version of the Bible, copyrighted 1946, 1952, © 1971, 1973 by
the Division of Christian Education of the National Council of the
Churches of Christ in the U.S.A., and are used by permission.

Copyright © 1978 by Thomas Nelson

All rights reserved under International and Pan-American Conven-
tions. Published in Nashville, Tennessee, by Thomas Nelson Inc.,
Publishers and simultaneously in Don Mills, Ontario, by Thomas
Nelson & Sons (Canada) Limited. Manufactured in the United States of
America.

Library of Congress Cataloging in Publication Data

Jones, Rufus, 1915–
  If I were in my thirties.

  Bibliography: p.
    1. Young adults—Religious life. 2. Christianity—
20th century. 3. Jones, Rufus, 1915–   I. Title.
BV4529.2.J66   248'.83   77–27398

Contents

1

Has the Salt Lost Its Taste?

"You chose a college a long way from home," I said to a young lady from New Jersey who was sitting next to me on the plane destined for Portland, Oregon. She replied that it was just the right distance. If it were any closer she would have to go home more often, and that, she said, would be more than she could take. She explained by saying, "I hate my parents."

Her story was one I heard many times during the turbulent sixties. Her mother and father were successful lawyers and spent most of their time pursuing their careers. They gave her all the spending money she wanted and she lived in luxury. But their money was not enough to make up for the love and affection she always desired but never received.

When she was old enough to want and need her mother's advice, mother was never at home. And when she was, she was too busy for the heart-to-heart talks with her daughter that other mothers and daughters enjoyed. Although there was usually someone older, perhaps a teacher, in whom she could confide, she always wished it could have been her mother.

She was attending a college where about eighty percent of the students were popping pills. Most of them had come from similar homes where they had encountered the same problems.

Although she was Jewish, she had made a commitment of her life to Jesus Christ. After her conversion, however, she was unable to find a church that satisfied her spiritual needs. She finally joined a very strict church on campus that forbade its members to maintain friendships with non-Christians. Such a restriction was a cause of conflict for her since she did not want to desert her unconverted friends.

We spent the rest of the flight discussing this and other problems Christians have as they relate to each other and to persons outside the church.

I could empathize with her as I too had belonged to a very strict fundamentalist church when I was in high school and college. I too had wanted to be accepted as a mature, dedicated Christian. At the same time, I had hesitated to cut myself off from the outside world.

This young lady was only one of many I talked with during the sixties who had problems relating to their parents, their churches, and their country—which was at that time involved in what they considered to be a cruel and unjust war.

They became aware of the injustice of segregation as they watched equal rights' demonstrations on television. Through their studies in social and political science they became disillusioned with the economic system. They saw that while it raised the average American's standard of living, it denied those same benefits to blacks and other minorities.

The television gave them a vivid picture of the horrors of war, and they did not want any part of the blood and violence for which they could see no purpose.

In their reaction to the materialism and competition

which they had seen destroy the values of their parents, they developed an alternative life-style. The youth counterculture was an attempt to dress and become like the poverty stricken minorities in order to identify with them in the battle against the system.

Students organized riots on campus, locked deans in their offices, and burned science laboratories that were subsidized by the military. They disrupted election campaigns and assaulted and taunted police when they tried to bring them under control.

Now most of the campus rebels of the 1960s are in their thirties and have become a part of the establishment they once had opposed. Some still bear the scars of the sixties—scars from which they may never completely recover. The generation now on campus is absorbed with the problems of personal survival in a world that no longer provides the security they have enjoyed as products of an affluent middle class—a class that is slowly disappearing as a result of increasing unemployment and the inflationary spiral.

Some of the one-time campus radicals have become disciples of Jesus Christ. They see in Him an example of One who cared and was willing to sacrifice His life in order to overcome prejudice and injustice—ills that are in many ways comparable to those in our present society.

Instead of trying to change things through violence and revolutionary tactics, these former young rebels are now preaching the gospel of the kingdom. They are also seeking to serve as models of an alternative life-style that rejects the values of this materialistic age and identifies with the poor and the oppressed.

Groups of Christians are buying clusters of houses in the inner-cities and undertaking communal-type living. This enables them to worship together and to encourage and support one another within a very difficult and rapidly deteriorating urban environment.

There are several magazines published by former radicals who are now Christians—some of these have rapidly growing circulations. They take a strong stand against violence, materialism, and the other evils they see in society. I refer to such magazines as *Sojourners, The Other Side,* and *The Wittenberg Door.*

I have come to know some of these young adults and admire them for their dedication to Jesus Christ and the compassion they have for the poor and the afflicted. They have strong convictions and are willing to act upon them. Through their publications they are doing much to awaken a growing number of evangelicals to the meaning of a dedicated and biblical discipleship in a changing world. I appreciate their stand for biblical truth and the contribution they are making to evangelicalism.

At the same time, I am concerned lest they become too simplistic in their approach to complex issues and go too far in separating themselves from the institutions of society. This was the fault of fundamentalists. They became so isolated from the culture while creating a fundamentalist counterculture that they ceased to serve as the salt of the earth and the light of the world.

On the other hand, I am concerned about modern evangelicalism which has reacted strongly against its fundamentalist heritage. It is in danger of repeating the error of liberalism: becoming so much a part of the culture that it is unable to serve as a corrective.

There are other young evangelicals with similar concerns for social justice who remain within the institutional structures. They are trying to effect change from within. Instead of withdrawing from the institutions of society as did the fundamentalists of my generation and as some of my young friends are doing today, they are seeking to penetrate society with the healing truth of Jesus Christ. They do not have any of the false illusions of the social gospel. They know a perfect kingdom of righteousness, justice, peace, and mercy cannot be established until the return of our Lord in all of His power and glory at the close of this age.

However, they do not see this as an excuse for the disciples of Christ to withdraw from the world or to compromise with the evil that is within it. They are very much aware of the sins and corruption that threaten to destroy the social, economic, political, and judicial systems of our nation. They do not profess to have a solution for all society's ills, but they are asking the right questions and seeking for honest answers. As they rise to positions of power and influence they are endeavoring to apply the Christian ethic as they understand it to every decision they make and every action they take.

These young persons are concerned about the apostate condition of the church and want to serve as instruments of renewal. They realize that it has not moved very far from the condition described by Kenneth L. Woodward in an article published in the sixties entitled "You Can't Find God in Church Anymore."[1] People still go to church, and the membership rolls are larger than ever. At the same time, the church seems to be making very little impact upon the individuals who belong to it or the culture of which they are a part.

Church attendance is near an all-time high, but so are guilt, anxiety, crime, violence, divorce, and dishonest business and professional practices. *U.S. News and World Report* recently revealed statistics on white-collar crime indicating that more than $40 billion annually is being stolen by people who live in white, middle-class suburbia. Many of these belong to churches and a surprising number would claim to have had a born-again experience.[2]

The reason for this apparent inconsistency becomes

[1]"You Can't Find God in Church Anymore," *Ladies Home Journal*, Mar. 1969.
[2]"A $40 Billion Crime Wave Swamps American Business," *U.S. News and World Report*, Feb. 21, 1977, pp. 47–48.

quite evident when we see the dichotomy one makes between his religious faith and his home or business practices. Many professing Christians do not seem to realize that faith is not just something to be verbalized in church. If it is genuine, faith determines how we make decisions in the home, at the office, in the voting booth, and in the marketplace. Our relationship with Jesus Christ should affect every word we speak, every action we take, and our attitudes toward racial and ethnic groups whose educations, cultures, and vocabularies are different from our own. Our faith should affect our attitude toward the material riches God entrusts to our care and toward the life-style we adopt. It should produce compassion and concern for the poor, for the mentally and physically handicapped, for those who are in prison, and for those who are victimized by crime and violence.

Being a true Christian means more than giving to a favorite charity or responding to some national or international disaster. It means a concern for the equitable distribution of the gross national product and a concern for how we share our food with a hungry world. "This people . . . honors me with their lips," God said through one of the ancient prophets, "but their heart is far from me" (Isa. 29:13).

The reason the twentieth-century church has failed to make an impact upon society, as it has done in former times and as it was intended to do when it was commissioned by our Lord, is its lack of concern for social justice. I believe this is because of the negative reaction to liberal theology that developed during the fundamentalist-modernist controversy which raged during the first half of this century.

If young adults could understand the important issues of that controversy and how each side felt the future of the gospel and the church was at stake, they would be able to view the situation with more charity and objectivity. That is not to excuse my generation for its un-charitable behavior. We need to overcome our emotional reaction and repent of the excessive anger and bitterness that characterized those on both sides of the debate. Until we do this, we cannot expect forgiveness and cleansing from God who loves us and gave His Son to die for us on the cross. God has commanded that we love each other and that we demonstrate our love not in words, but in deeds and in truth. It is only as this love is produced in our lives through the power of the Holy Spirit, and as a result of our faith, that we can be sure we have eternal life.

Not only are young adults concerned about the materialism, racism, and legalism that still exist within the church, but they are also concerned about the lack of love and zeal for God. Our church services are often cold, formal, and ritualistic and our singing is merely a repetition of words that once stirred the emotions of great congregations. Our prayers are said in a perfunctory manner with very little consciousness that they are being addressed to the God of the universe who is present in our sanctuaries. Sermons are often filled with pious platitudes that are soon forgotten after the service as we talk with fellow church members about the things of this world that take priority in our lives.

Even when we do pray with earnestness to God, He doesn't always seem to be listening. Sometimes we feel we are in a time similar to the one described by Hosea when he said of Israel, "With their flocks and herds they shall go to seek the Lord, but they will not find him; he has withdrawn from them" (Hos. 5:6).

Young adults today are aware that something is wrong with the church and they are not sure what it is, but they want to know.

"If you were in your thirties, and you had your present understanding of the world situation and the condition that exists within the church, what would you do?" I am in my early sixties. This question was presented to me by a group of young men who are in their thirties.

I replied to their question by saying, "I would seek to establish a continuity with the past through a study of history and how it has affected and shaped the present. I would also establish from the Scriptures a hope for the future, for this also would have an effect upon my attitude and what I would do in the present. When I had done this, I would give my attention to an in-depth study of the present trends and seek to discern between those that are temporary and passing and those that will remain long enough to affect the future. Jesus said to an audience He was addressing, 'You know how to interpret the appearance of the sky, but you cannot interpret the signs of the times' " (Matt. 16:3).

We need to project some of the present trends into the future and see how it will be changed and shaped by them. Then we can develop plans and programs that will enable us to present the unchanging and biblical gospel in a relevant manner.

First we need to take a sweeping view of what has become known as the Modern Age of Science and Reason. It began with the Renaissance and lasted until the mid-1960s. We shall see how the ideas that proceeded from the Renaissance and Reformation periods resulted in the French and American revolutions as well as in the colonial revivals and the rise of theological modernism.

Next, we shall look at the fundamentalist-modernist controversy and see how it has produced the apostasy so evident in the churches today. An understanding of the results of this controversy will explain the cold, formal, and ritualistic worship services of many mainline churches, their declining memberships, and their secular solutions to spiritual problems. It will explain the materialism and the employment of business principles and Madison Avenue techniques in modern forms of evangelism and promotion of church growth. Knowledge of the past is the only basis for understanding these present occurrences. Young evangelicals with this knowledge should be able to understand, though not excuse, the present resistance of the church to their proposed changes.

After we have looked into the past, we shall examine the Good News concerning the future kingdom and see how this kingdom has already broken into history and become a part of the present.

We will then examine the problems and opportunities of the new global culture that is emerging as a result of the technological and economic advances of the Third World.

The church of Jesus Christ will be able to penetrate this new culture the same as Jesus and the apostles penetrated the newly emerging culture of their era and as the leaders of the Reformation created the religious foundation for Western civilization.

2

The Result of Rationalism

"I have been praying all week for God to give me a message for this chapel period and my prayers have gone unanswered," announced a professor as he stood in the pulpit of a college chapel in the late 1960s. "It seems as though the heavens are brass or else that God is not there. I could talk about some subject for the time allotted to me but it would not be a message from God. Therefore, I think it would be better for me to sit down." And he did.

His honest confession may have been one of the most effective messages ever given in that chapel, for many of the students were having a similar experience in their devotional lives. The depression and despair of the secular campuses were reaching into the Christian colleges, marking the end of an era referred to previously which began with the Renaissance and continued through the first half of the twentieth century. It was called the Age of Science and Reason, during which time we were to believe that slowly but surely humanity was overcoming its fears and superstitions.

The belief in man's inevitable improvement and progress is supported by the theory of evolution made popular by Charles Darwin in his book *The Origin of the Species*, first published in 1859. Evolution quickly became the hypothesis not only for biology and anthropology but for the social sciences as well. Man,* it was believed, had come of age and was no longer dependent upon God as an answer to the ultimate questions people ask or for the control of the forces of nature. It was believed that as man would become more enlightened regarding the laws of the universe, he would be able to predict and even change nature's course in order to serve the welfare of society as a whole and the individual units of society in particular.

This kind of thinking began to dominate the minds of scholars teaching in the great universities of the late nineteenth century and gradually filtered down to the masses, most of whom were uneducated and still believed in the supernatural. Today, the theory of evolution is widely accepted as fact even among some Christians.

Looking back further in history, we see the beginnings of individualism and democracy. The Reformation was an attempt by theologians to defend and propagate the Christian gospel among those who were endeavoring to throw off the yoke of a state church that persecuted and even put to death those who advocated the enlightened views of the Renaissance. The Roman church had used its power to hinder and stifle any teaching contrary to its theology, which was based in part on ideas of the Greek philosophers concerning the cosmos. This theology was supported by proof texts from the Bible that were often misinterpreted or removed from their context to make them fit the ideas proposed by the theologians and philosophers of the period.

When Renaissance thought began to spread, the the-

*The term "man" is used here and elsewhere in a generic sense and is not meant to exclude women.

ology of the church was challenged. The reformers reexamined the Bible and developed a theology permitting more freedom within the church for individual expression. The new freedom included not only religion but also extended to social, economic, and political views. The pope in Rome began to lose much of his political power. All of this culminated in the birth of democratic government and free enterprise in business.

The rebellion did not stop with Rome, however, for there were those who claimed the reformers did not go far enough. So the Ana-Baptists, Puritans, Methodists, and Congregationalists separated from the reformed churches in the interest of more freedom from government and a biblical life-style in keeping with that desired freedom.

The move toward freedom continued when the left-wing evangelical churches in America were established. They threw off the yoke of the Puritan congregational and Anglican churches, which had politically dominated the American territories in much the same way the Roman church had dominated Europe before the Reformation.

The colonial revivals, initiated through Jonathan Edwards's preaching, emphasized the need for an individual conversion experience that included repentance, confession, forsaking of sins, and a genuine change in attitude and behavior. Edwards and his followers condemned the cold, dead orthodoxy of the dominant churches and as a result were excluded from their membership. They found the kind of fellowship that fit their new experience in the Methodist, Baptist, and Presbyterian churches.

Robert Bellah, in his book *The Broken Covenant*, states that the original Constitution, which provided for liberty and justice for all, was made possible by the colonial revivals.[1] In spite of the high ideals of the Constitution,

[1]Robert Bellah, *The Broken Covenant* (New York: Seabury Press, 1975), p. 62.

however, it did not protect Indians and black slaves who were denied the status of citizenship. This had to wait for the second great awakening, which, according to Bellah, began with the preaching of Charles Finney and resulted in the Emancipation Proclamation that freed the slaves. Neither one of these advances was made without violence. The first resulted from the Revolutionary War and the second in the Civil War. He calls these America's first and second great times of trial.

The third great awakening, Bellah says, began in the 1960s and may lead to what he calls "America's third great time of trial," just as the others did.[2] The present spiritual renewal, like the other two, began with dissatisfaction with a church that had become cold, formal, ritualistic, and worldly. Such churches had so accommodated themselves to the world that their values had become more cultural than biblical. They had lost their sense of mission and purpose and also the sense of God's presence and power.

The article, "You Can't Find God in Church Anymore," mentioned in the first chapter, expressed the way many people were feeling about the worship services they were attending—the college chapel service is an example. Not many pastors have had the courage to admit that their sermons were not from God, but they have been aware that something was wrong, and so have the members of their congregations.

A young man who was present in the chapel service mentioned earlier later admitted to a Sunday School class for young adults the despair that he and others like him were experiencing. The young man told why he was a Christian existentialist. After he had been with the class for four Sundays, they asked me to speak to them for four class periods and to explain why students felt as they did about their parents and the institutions of society. Why were their values so different from those of their parents? What could they do to avoid the alienation

[2]*Ibid.*

of their children from themselves and from society? I did not promise clear-cut answers, but I was interested in exploring the problem with them.

I related to these young adults that my rapport with college students had grown out of a common interest in the socioeconomic problems the social engineers had failed to solve for minority groups. Often students invited me to their apartments for lengthy rap sessions. Our discussions included not only the problems of society but also the resistance to change on the part of their parents and churches. I could understand their compassion for the poor and the oppressed minority groups. In fact, I welcomed their concern, for I had been preaching against the sins of our white middle-class society and the silence of the churches since the mid-fifties. I had become aware of the injustice of segregation and discrimination against blacks and other minorities as a result of my involvement in a ministry to the cities of America.

However, while I shared their convictions as to what should be done, I differed in the method of how these goals should be accomplished. I did not become involved in demonstrations or political activity because I believe social problems result from spiritual problems and can only be solved by an appeal to the conscience of white middle-class Americans, most of whom belong to a church or synagogue. If those who profess to believe in the God of the Bible would practice His principles in their social, business, and political involvements, I believe we could eliminate injustice and discrimination against blacks and other minorities.

Nonviolent tactics were an attempt by civil rights demonstrators to reach the conscience of white Americans. Christians, of all people, should have been the first to respond—but they were frequently the last. I shared the students' disappointment in this regard. However, I did not understand nor appreciate the violence that erupted on campus nor the complete despair and hysteria that followed their failure to obtain instant justice.

I pointed out to the class that part of the problem resulted from television. They had seen John Wayne come to the rescue of anyone victimized by injustice and solve the problem before the ten o'clock news. They thought they could do the same thing, but they soon discovered it doesn't happen so easily or quickly in real life. The depression and despair of students when their revolution failed went beyond their idealistic concerns for the poor and the oppressed, however, and developed into personal problems that involved their mental health and emotional stability. Many of them developed suicidal tendencies and more than four thousand were taking their own lives each year;[3] thousands of others have been or will be destroyed by drugs.

A book by a twenty-one-year-old Harvard student named Steven Kelmar illustrates this tendency toward despair by campus radicals. Entitled *Push Comes to Shove*, it describes this young man's experience during the Harvard riots. He was head of the campus Socialist party and at the same time wrote for *The New York Times*. Eventually, a group of young radicals known as the "Weathermen" infiltrated and took over the party and soon it became the source of violence on campus. Kelmar describes some of the party members as brilliant students who became depressed, addicted to hard drugs, and soon began to deteriorate physically and mentally. For many, life no longer had any meaning or purpose.[4]

To gain an understanding of the results of alienation within society, I reread *Varieties of Religious Experience* by William James and shared his findings with the class. He describes other periods of mass depression. He tells of Tolstoy, who at the height of his career and without any apparent reason, developed a compulsion to commit suicide and had to eliminate all knives or ropes from his

[3]Francene Klagsbrun, "Teen-age Suicide," *Family Circle*, Apr. 5, 1977, p. 44.
[4]Steven Kelmar, *Push Comes to Shove* (Boston: Houghton Mifflin Co., 1970).

home. A Christian conversion experience brought him out of his depression and changed his entire outlook on life.[5]

My mind went back to the colonial revivals, each of which was preceded by a similar time of depression, hysteria, and suicide. This led me to believe we had come to the end of an era of rationalism. What we were witnessing among the students, I said, was a prelude to another great spiritual awakening. Based upon my study of the past, I informed the class, "It will not start with the church because the church is not aware of its apostate condition. But it will begin among the most alienated group in our society." I then named the hippies in California as the most likely people to experience revival. Two years later *Look* magazine published an article about the conversion of the hippies in California—they were known as "Jesus freaks."[6] I told the class that when the revival came, the churches would be severely critical of it, and of course, this is what happened. Now, as I predicted, these young Christians are infiltrating and having an influence upon a few churches and parachurch organizations.

However, unlike the revivals that began with Edwards and Finney, the present converts are not making the impact I had anticipated. I am still hopeful. I trust that our churches will come alive with spiritual vitality and that we will see a demonstration of the dynamic power of the gospel, not only to change the lives of individuals, but through them to bring about necessary social, economic, and political changes within our nation. There are some signs that this is beginning to happen. If so, God's hand of judgment may be withheld from our country. It is our only chance of recovery from the losses already suffered because of our lack of obedi-

[5]William James, *Varieties of Religious Experience* (New York: MacMillan Publishing Co., Inc., 1961).
[6]Brian Vachon, "The Jesus Movement Is Upon Us," *Look*, Feb. 9, 1971, p. 15ff.

ence to God and our departure from the righteousness and justice He requires of nations as well as of individuals.

Every revival has been criticized by the established churches because of the highly charged emotional atmosphere that prevails among some of its converts. We are not without an example of this today. The contemporary church renewal movement has caused skepticism among traditional evangelicals, especially in regard to the ecstatic experiences of many new converts.

However, if the established churches would understand that gifts of the Spirit are a part of revival and would receive new converts without being turned off by their effervescence, they could profit greatly from these Christians, and their own members would be renewed in the process. However, if they are unable to recognize and welcome the supernatural work of the Holy Spirit, new structures will be formed and the old will be left to gradually fade away or continue the struggle for survival.

It is important, however, to discern that which is of the flesh from that which is of the Spirit. If converts are content to base their salvation on experience alone and do not soon begin to feed upon the meat of the Word and live according to the righteousness and justice of God's kingdom, they soon will find themselves back in the world. It would be better for them not to have known the way of righteousness than after having known it to turn back from the holy commandment delivered to them (see 2 Pet. 2:21, 22). They are compared by Peter to a sow that after being washed returns to wallowing in the mud. There are signs, however, that many of the new converts are growing in the Lord and are seeking to obey His commands.

Rationalism, which denies the spiritual and emotional needs of humanity, always ends in despair and depression. Existentialism, which recognizes the importance of the emotional and spiritual nature of man, makes a similar mistake when it denies that we are also rational beings. There must be a balance between the rational, emotional, and spiritual in order for a person to be all God meant for him to be. The person whose life is fully surrendered to God will live not for himself but for others whom God would have him serve.

We have come to the end of an era that began with an unrealistic and unbiblical faith in man. It developed a naive optimism concerning what could be accomplished by man's efforts apart from the intervention of God. As a result, it ended in the disillusionment and despair of the sixties and the skepticism of the seventies. Today the students on campus are known for their apathy toward all forms of idealism. Generally, they reflect the materialistic and hedonistic values of their parents. They are concerned about good grades and getting a job when they graduate.

At the same time, the problems of our society continue to fester and multiply. Racial inequality and prejudice, if allowed to continue, will eventually lead to a major confrontation. The blacks are now joined by the Chicanos, Indians, Puerto Ricans, and other ethnic minorities in their discontent. They are at present as divided from each other as they are from the predominant white middle class. But if they should ever settle their differences and get together, I believe we could have another Civil War in the United States.

It is important, therefore, that we pause to review our past, make a thorough study of the present, and seek to provide some answers for the future. The social scientists who were so sure they had all the answers have seen the failure of one program after another. They are now puzzled and do not know what to do. We have in the past believed in the power of the president of the United States to provide solutions to our complex problems. We believed that if we could only get the right man in the White House, he would inspire and lead the nation out of its problems and into the promised land.

President Franklin D. Roosevelt brought a spirit of hope and optimism in the midst of the 1929 depression with his promise of a "new deal" for the common man. President Harry Truman promised a "square deal" and President John Kennedy talked about "new frontiers." He gathered around him the "best and the brightest" and they gave us the Bay of Pigs fiasco and led us into a deeper involvement in Vietnam, which resulted in war and all the tragedies of the period following his assassination. President Lyndon Johnson promised the "Great Society" and began with a war on poverty. Being distracted from the war on poverty by the war in Vietnam, Johnson ended up losing both wars and consequently the chance for reelection. President Richard Nixon gave us Watergate and was too involved with that to be concerned about the deteriorating cities and the plight of the poor. President Gerald Ford made a good transition president; now the world is carefully watching President Jimmy Carter. Many people, however, are still skeptical of the executive branch with its accompanying bureaucracy. There is an underlying fear that we have created something that has gone beyond our control and that very little, if anything, can be done to change its course.

There is one thing we do know: a sovereign God is still on His throne. A genuine spiritual awakening can make a difference and if I were in my thirties today, I would pray and work for the renewal of the church that will enable it to provide spiritual solutions for the problems that plague us.

3

The Church
Changed
by Conflict

A general overview of history is important for an understanding of the present, but we also need a more detailed study of the relationship of the way we think and act now to our more recent past. Those who ignore history are not necessarily bound to repeat its mistakes, but some mistakes might be avoided if we are aware of the influence of past ideas and events on our present philosophy and pattern of living.

Young people raised in poverty, for example, are not as quick to condemn the values of our materialistic society as those who have always enjoyed the security and luxuries of the affluent middle class. Knowledge of the Depression and its effects upon a whole generation would have helped the generation of the sixties understand not only the values of their parents but also the gap that existed between themselves and the people of the inner cities with whom they were trying to identify. By giving up their affluent life-styles, they merely assuaged their consciences but did not help to make it possible for the poor to enjoy the comforts and luxuries they had never known.

The same principle applies to the churches and their failure to meet the expectations of the youth during the sixties and even the more biblically oriented youth of the seventies. To understand the failure of the church to serve as both a proclaimer of God's Word and a defender of social justice during this critical era through which we are now passing, we must have an adequate understanding of the fundamentalist-modernist controversy which raged during the first half of this century.

When we understand the importance that each side in this controversy placed on the ideals for which it stood and the effects these ideals would have on the future of the church and its influence upon the world, it is difficult to place the blame squarely on one side or the other. Each side took an important aspect of the gospel and emphasized it to the exclusion of the rest of the gospel. As the battle progressed, a new generation was born who came to think that whichever emphasis it sided with was the whole gospel instead of a part.

As a result, both sides were right in what they affirmed and wrong in what they denied. The modernist was wrong in denying the essential doctrines of the Christian faith, which include the divine inspiration and authority of Scripture, the virgin birth, the Resurrection, and the second coming of Christ. He was right in his emphasis upon the social and ethical teachings of Christ, the apostles, and the prophets. The fundamentalist was right in defending the basic doctrines of the Christian faith, but wrong in denying the social and ethical implications of that faith.

These two positions became solidified after the death of the original leaders. Walter Rauschenbusch, usually referred to as the father of the social gospel, believed in the necessity of an individual conversion experience that would result in a social concern. William Jennings Bryan, the most prominent spokesman for the fundamentals of the faith, was also bold in declaring the socio-economic implications of these doctrines.

It was during the thirties and forties that the overreaction of fundamentalism to the modernist error caused them to move away from the biblical gospel. The fundamentalists devised a simplified formula defending their position that was supported by proof texts removed from their scriptural contexts. As a result, neither modernists nor fundamentalists were preaching the whole gospel of the kingdom as taught by Jesus and the apostles.

"I do not believe in the virgin birth of Jesus, and I do not know of a man with any intelligence who does." Those words were written by Harry Emerson Fosdick in answer to a letter from a pastor who had been told Dr. Fosdick did believe in the virgin birth and had asked for his confirmation.[1]

Although Fosdick was the most articulate spokesman for what became known as modernist theology, he did not come from a liberal home or church. As a boy, he was a member of the Prospect Avenue Baptist Church in Buffalo, New York, where his father led the singing. It was a church that believed in the full inspiration and authority of Scripture, including the doctrine of creation, the fall of man, and his need for redemption through the death of Christ on the cross. The miracles of the Bible including the virgin birth, the Resurrection, and the second coming of Christ were taught. The Prospect Church still has an active ministry and is preaching the same basic doctrines of the historic faith that it did when Fosdick's family were members. Fosdick, in his autobiography, speaks warmly and lovingly of the faith

[1]George Dollar, *A History of Fundamentalism* (Greenville, S.C.: Bob Jones University Press, 1973), p. 101.

of his parents and the closely knit fellowship and love they enjoyed as a family.

It was not until he entered Colgate University that he began to seriously question the authenticity of the Scriptures. His first letters home were filled with the thrills and wonders of his new environment. Fosdick said at Colgate he "found what I needed most—the impact of some very stimulating personalities."[2] His first year on campus was a good one. There was nothing in the religious life of the village church or the campus to disturb the even tenor of his accustomed thinking. He had no premonitions of the explosion that was to follow. He did become a convinced believer in evolution and thought he might shock his family when he announced his new discovery during Sunday dinner after he arrived home for his first vacation. There was a dead silence when he made his announcement and then a response that he said "took the wind out of my sails" from his father who replied, "Well, I believed that before you were born."

As he returned to college, other questions arose concerning the structure of religious thought in which Fosdick had been reared. "The fundamentalists in later years have hated me plentifully," he wrote, "but I started out as one of them."[3] Just when the crack in the old structure began, he was not quite sure, but he said it probably started with the story of Samson and the other miracle stories of the Bible. During his second year at Colgate, he was rebelling against what he called the bibliolatry and theology he had been taught in his youth. His struggle was mental rather than moral. When he left for college at the beginning of his junior year, he told his mother, "I'll behave as though there were a God, but mentally I'm going to clear God out of the universe and start all over to see what I can find."[4]

[2]Harry E. Fosdick, *The Living of These Days: An Autobiography* (New York: Harper and Row, 1956), p. 48.

[3]*Ibid.*, p. 49.

[4]*Ibid.*, p. 51.

I include this part of Fosdick's background and his struggle in making the transition from fundamentalism to modernism because his experience was typical of so many students of that era. I went through some of the same questioning and doubts in my own quest for truth. Fortunately, I developed a close friendship with the godly pastor of a Presbyterian church who had a logically sharp mind and had majored in apologetics. He taught a class once a week for students who were faced with questions and inconsistencies between conservative theology and scientific *theories* being taught as proven *facts*.

If I were in my thirties today, I would want to have a similar class for students with intellectual struggles during which we would discuss their doubts and the imagined discrepancies between science and the Bible.

Fosdick said his junior year at college was his most enjoyable. But it was also a time for critical examination of his religious beliefs. "There was no thought," he said, "of returning to old positions, but I began to see the possibility of new positions—old spiritual values in new categories."[5] He received help in this regard from Professor William Newton Clarke, of Colgate's theological seminary. "Here," he said, "was an honest man saying what he really thought, defying the obscurantism of old opinions and daring to phrase the Christian faith in the categories of modern thinking."[6]

At the end of his junior year, Fosdick decided to be a minister. When one of his professors heard about his choice he asked, "Has it ever occurred to you that a minister is to be an exponent of the spiritual life?" The professor was right, for Fosdick was headed for the ministry without the faintest interest in any sect or denomination and, by his own admission, he could not have told clearly what he believed about any major doctrine.

[5]*Ibid.*, p. 54.
[6]*Ibid.*

When he entered divinity school in 1900, the development of a "new theology" was well underway. The old Calvinism was giving way during the nineties, even in the theological seminaries. The results of biblical criticism were being imported to America from Britain and Germany. As a result, such doctrines as the Trinity were not seen to be in the Bible at all.

"The trouble," said Fosdick, "was that historical scholarship did find in the Bible ideas no longer scientifically credible, but it did not find in the Bible certain ideas which had become Christian orthodoxy."[7] Under the influence of men like George Hegel, Rudolf Lotze, and Friedrich Schleimacher, philosophical idealism powerfully affected American theology in the nineteenth century. The old foundations of biblical authority were shaken and Christian experience became more and more the "factual" basis for theology.

The new liberal theology, as might be expected, set off a reaction from those who continued to believe in the historic doctrines of the Christian faith; the controversy of the century had begun. As early as 1910, two wealthy businessmen furnished the money for the publication of a series of books called *The Fundamentals*.[8] Each chapter was written by a different author defending what was believed by conservative Christians to be essential to the Christian faith. These books were sent to every pastor and YMCA worker in the United States. Later the word "fundamentalist" was coined by *The Watchman Examiner* to describe those who believed in the fundamental doctrines of Christianity.[9]

During the first two decades of the twentieth century, the conflict between liberal and conservative Christians moved toward a climax. When the storm did break,

[7]*Ibid.*, p. 55.

[8]A. C. Dixon, ed., *The Fundamentals* (Chicago: Testimony, 1912).

[9]The term "fundamentalist" was probably first used in an editorial by Curtis Lee Lawes, circa 1920. Lawes was editor of the *Examiner*, an independent paper written for the conservative element of the Northern Baptist Convention.

Fosdick was in the center. His sermon entitled "Shall the Fundamentalist Win?" stated the differences of conviction dividing the two groups on such matters as the virgin birth of Jesus, the inerrancy of the Scriptures, and the second coming of Christ. This attack upon both the doctrines of the fundamentalists and their Christian character was published by a liberal Presbyterian layman, the head of a large publicity organization. It was distributed throughout the country and the battle was on that was to last through the next three decades. During this time all but two of the major Protestant denominations came under the control of liberal leadership. The two exceptions were The Southern Baptist Convention and The Missouri Synod of the Lutheran Church. The latter has recently had its problems, but in this case the conservatives have remained in control and the liberals have been forced to leave—just the opposite of the results of the earlier controversy in other denominations, and indicating the change that has taken place in the mood of the country since World War II.

The fundamentalist response to Fosdick's sermon was led by Dr. Clarence McCartney, then minister of a Presbyterian church in Philadelphia. Fosdick was a Baptist minister serving as pastor of a Presbyterian church in New York. The fundamentalists demanded to know why the presbytery was allowing a Baptist to preach doctrines contrary to the Westminster Confession of Faith in a Presbyterian church.

The 1923 General Assembly of the Presbyterian Church was presented with resolutions from ten presbyteries demanding that Fosdick's heretical preaching be stopped. William Jennings Bryan was one of the leading figures of the assembly and his oratory helped to achieve the fundamentalist victory. By a vote of 439 to 359, a minority report was adopted expressing profound sorrow that doctrines contrary to the standards of the church were being proclaimed in the Old First Pulpit and directing the Presbytery of New York to take such action "as will require the preaching and teaching in the First Presbyterian Church of New York City to conform to the system of doctrine in the confession of faith."[10] The report specified five doctrines: (1) the inerrant Bible; (2) the virgin birth; (3) the substitutionary atonement of Jesus' death as "a sacrifice to satisfy divine justice"; (4) the physical resurrection; and (5) Christ's supernatural miracles. Upon hearing the General Assembly's decision, Fosdick presented his resignation to the church. It was accepted by the congregation after some delay.

When Fosdick moved from the Presbyterian church back into the Baptist fold, he found himself in a similar storm of controversy. The Baptists held a series of meetings of their own. At the opening session, Dr. John Roach Straton, pastor of Calvary Baptist Church, New York, said he had "come to the conclusion that Dr. Fosdick is not only a Baptist bootlegger, but he is also a Presbyterian outlaw: without the slightest ill will and with no desire to injure him personally, I nevertheless declare, in the light of Bible teaching and in the name of eternal truth, that Dr. Harry Emerson Fosdick is a religious outlaw—he is the Jesse James of the theological world."[11]

It would be a misrepresentation to say that the Christian community was sharply divided into only two groups. There were all sorts of liberals and all sorts of fundamentalists. Most liberals were not nearly so modernistic as their foes pictured them, and most fundamentalists were not nearly so pugnaciously reactionary as the liberals made them out to be. Even Fosdick admitted with respect and gratitude that there were staunch conservatives who did not agree with his opinions but who were gracious, fair-minded, and courteous. The same can be said for some of the staunch liberals. As the

[10]Fosdick, *The Living of These Days*, p. 148.
[11]*Ibid.*, p. 153.

controversy went on, however, and angry passions became overheated, the vocabulary of invectives often became unrestrained.

Liberalism reached its zenith during World War II. Even prior to that time, there were those from within the liberal camp who were developing serious doubts about some of their basic presuppositions. In 1935, Fosdick preached another famous sermon entitled "We Must Go Beyond Modernism." In this address he said, "We have adapted and adjusted and accommodated and conceded long enough. We have at times gotten so low down that we talked as though the highest compliment that could be paid to almighty God was that a few scientists believed in Him."[12]

Young persons need to heed what Fosdick was saying in this sermon. Are we not as evangelicals in danger of making the same mistake when we feature the football heroes, prominent politicians, television and movie personalities, and Miss Americas in our evangelistic crusades and Christian periodicals? Is the highest compliment we can pay God the fact that these famous personalities profess to believe in Him? Is this the proper motivating factor in a person's decision to commit his or her life to Christ?

Do not misunderstand. I appreciate their stand for Christ and their witness for Him. But I think we must be aware of the danger in appealing to people to join the church for worldly and selfish reasons rather than because a life-transforming commitment has been made to Jesus as the Person to whose lordship we want to submit and of whose teaching we want to obey.

If I were in my thirties today, I would seek to avoid the charge that Fosdick makes against his liberal colleagues when he declares,

To many of its adherents, liberalism became a static orthodoxy; it dug in its heels where it was and merely stood its ground; it

[12]*Ibid.*, p. 245.

failed to see that the admonition "new occasions teach new duties" applies not to reactionaries alone but to modernists also. . . . In order to move out into the terrific post-war generation with a gospel suited to man's staggering needs it did not have to surrender a single one of its staggering gains, but it did have to wake up, recognizing that reactionary liberalism can be as much a failure as reactionary traditionalism.[13]

The same can be said of conservative evangelicalism. Liberalism won the *battle* for control of the denominations but they lost the *war*. Conservative churches are now growing while liberal churches are dying. I am happy about the growth of evangelicalism, but I am frightened at the same time.

The most dangerous period in the church's life is the time of its greatest popularity. My generation, for the most part, has accommodated itself to the present culture. Some of those who have led the evangelical advance since World War II, and who from a human viewpoint deserve most of the credit for the popularity and success the church now enjoys, have failed to see that the necessary reaction to the excesses of both liberalism and fundamentalism should not be frozen into a static pattern, but that it is time for us to move on to the tremendous opportunities that are before us in the late seventies and early eighties.

The counsel offered to the avant-garde of the fifties also applies to the leaders that have developed from the youth counterculture movement of the sixties. Many of them are still fighting the battles of that era while failing to see, as we enter the third century of American life, the new issues to which we must apply the gospel of Jesus Christ. The power of the Holy Spirit to change the lives of those who control the structures of society and who determine the kind of world that we shall establish for the future is waiting to be unleashed.

After World War II, fundamentalists, along with other

[13]*Ibid.*, p. 248.

middle-class white Anglo-Saxons, became a part of the affluent society. This enabled us to upgrade our Bible institutes, changing them to Bible colleges and later to liberal arts colleges. We also started new seminaries and began to place a higher priority on education. Pastors became refined and their messages became more positive and less legalistic and judgmental.

While the new pastors were just as loyal to the fundamental doctrines as the old, they no longer wanted to be identified as fundamentalists because of the bad connotations associated with the word. Instead, they chose to call themselves "conservatives" or "evangelicals." Either of these terms would distinguish them from the extremists among the fundamentalists and the unitarians among the liberals. The term "conservative" later became associated with right-wing politics, and so today most describe themselves as evangelicals. Evangelicals have been highly successful during the third quarter of this century and, without dispute, boast that a majority of the pastors and lay persons within Protestantism adhere to the essentials of the Christian faith.

During the third quarter of this century, Billy Graham has preached to congregations of thousands at one time both in the United States and in other countries. He has been highly respected by presidents and other political leaders and has often been called to consult with them during times of crisis. We have seen the growth and development of large churches, some with memberships that total from ten to twenty thousand. Many other achievements were accomplished during this era.

While I rejoice in the growth of evangelicalism, I am at the same time concerned about the seeming lack of spiritual depth and understanding of the gospel as revealed in the Scriptures. We have become so absorbed with the desire to show visible and measurable growth that we have unconsciously compromised the gospel in order to make it more popular with the masses. In our reaction to the hell-fire and damnation preaching for which we were once criticized, we have gone to the other extreme and become so positive that many of us no longer preach against the sins people commit; neither do we expect to see visible evidence of repentance. People are asked only to acknowledge that we are all sinners and to believe that Jesus died for us and then to pray a little prayer asking Him to save us. While it is true that we are sinners and it was necessary for Christ to die on the cross in order for God to save us, we are never told in Scripture that by praying a little prayer we can be saved.

According to the teaching of Jesus and the apostles, salvation requires genuine repentance and confession of sin and then there must be a sincere commitment to the lordship of Jesus Christ in every area of life and in all social relationships. The evidence of a genuine faith is the works that result from it.

4

The Future Enters the Present

In his book *The Human Prospect*, Robert Heilbroner begins with the question, "Is there any hope for man?" Before he comes to the end of the first chapter, he gives his answer in one word—no.[1]

He declares that the future is nothing but a continuation of the darkness, cruelty, and disorder of the past. He supports his position by calling attention to the problems of an increasing population, the inability to produce enough food to keep masses of people from starving, and the possibility of a nuclear war that within a brief time could destroy the major cities of the world. He supports these predictions with both statistics and logic.

Heilbroner is not alone in his pessimism concerning prospects for the future. He is merely adding his voice to

[1]Robert Heilbroner, *An Inquiry into the Human Prospect* (W. W. Norton and Co., 1974).

those of other intellectuals who see the world as being on the brink of disaster. What a contrast to the "inevitability of human progress" so ardently believed by the intellectuals of only a few years ago.

If Heilbroner and the other doomsday philosophers are right, there is no hope for the future and life has no meaning or purpose. When we lose all hope for the future, we are left with nothing but despair in the present.

It is said that Martin Heidegger (1889-   ) would warn the beginning students of his classes about the temptation to commit suicide once they had mastered the true meaning of his existential philosophy. Pessimism regarding the future is an outgrowth of this same philosophical stance.

Why should I or anyone else spend time and energy trying to convince people to lay aside their prejudices, to forsake unethical practices in their businesses or professions, and to establish a more just and equitable society if there is no meaning or purpose to life?

Our motivation as Christians is the Good News of the kingdom and the hope that it provides for the future. Not only is our present determined by the ideas and events of the past, but it is also shaped by the hope that our faith in Christ provides for the age to come.

There is a new order ahead which will be ushered in by our Lord Jesus Christ when He returns. There will be no crying in that kingdom, for there will be no pain, sorrow, or death—only the righteous (those who live by faith in Christ) will be allowed to enter. Those who practice sorcery, idolatry, sexual sins, and murder will not be allowed to enter, nor will those who love and practice falsehood.

This kingdom will be devoid of people who are going along with those business and professional practices that are in utter conflict with the gospel. The Scriptures warn that the kingdom of God will exclude those who practice deceit or who take bribes from the rich to pass laws that discriminate against the poor and oppressed minorities. It will exclude those who pay less than a fair wage to their employees or who use discrimination in their hiring and promotion of people because of race, sex, or other superficial reasons. Wheelers and dealers who put aside ethical considerations to make a fast buck *are already* separated from those who will enter the new order, which God has prepared for those who love and serve Him.

You see, the kingdom of God is *not only a future event* that takes place in the age to come, but it *has already broken into history*. Those who have been born again belong to the kingdom now. The Lord Jesus reigns today over His people in the church, and this present reign is but a foretaste of the glory to come. We shall receive eternal life at the close of this age and we have *already* been given a new quality of life on earth as a result of our faith in Jesus. This is why God calls for righteousness *now!*

The rich young ruler introduced in Mark 10 asked our Lord, "What must I do to inherit eternal life?" Jesus replied, "Go, sell what you have, and give to the poor . . . and come, follow me." The ruler went away sorrowful for he did not want to part with his possessions. Yet he longed for eternal life. Jesus said with a sympathetic sigh, "How hard it will be for those who have riches to enter the kingdom of God!"

Those who have eternal life enter the kingdom. The kingdom is a new order, the ideal society God has promised for the future. It is also a present reality for the disciples of Christ who have been "delivered . . . from the dominion of darkness and transferred . . . to the kingdom of his beloved Son in whom we have redemption, the forgiveness of sins" (Col. 1:13).

The kingdom of God exists side by side with the kingdom of Satan. They are two conflicting forces in the world. We as humans have been brought into the conflict and we are forced to take sides with one or the other. We are either for Christ or anti-Christ; there is no neutral ground.

The disciples of Christ are in the world but they are not of it. They are strangers and pilgrims passing through on their way to the Promised Land.

But if we are to avoid the self-destruction predicted by men like Heilbroner, there must be a complete change in the life-styles that characterize the people of our nation. As Christians, our hope gives us *reason* to change. Christians are to serve as ambassadors who proclaim and live out His message of reconciliation between man and God and between man and man. Consider the solution in the Sermon on the Mount (Matt. 5). "Blessed are the peacemakers," Jesus said, "for they shall be called the sons of God" (v. 9). *We* are the ones who are to serve as mediators during a time when warring factions are trying to destroy each other.

"Blessed are the merciful for they shall obtain mercy" (v. 7). A disciple of Jesus Christ should not try to avenge those who do him wrong. Rather he should remember the mercy God has shown him when he deserved judgment and consequently act in mercy toward others.

"Blessed are the pure in heart for they shall see God" (v. 8). The believer should not be dishonest or devious in his ways. He is not to devise evil plans but he is to be kind, gentle, and without guile.

"Blessed are those who hunger and thirst for righteousness, for they shall be satisfied" (v. 6). Righteousness is mentioned three times in the Sermon. According to Jesus, those who live for righteousness' sake will be persecuted, just as the Old Testament prophets were persecuted. Jesus Christ Himself was crucified because the righteousness and justice He proclaimed provoked prideful, rebellious sinners.

But note carefully, not only will we suffer persecution

within the world system when we take a stand for righteousness, but we will soon find that there are people in the religious system who are filled with hatred for what is right as well. To call dishonest and unrighteous practices into question is to infer that those who do such things are not Christians. Those who are exposed when light is shed upon wrongdoing often become angry and try to discredit the person who calls attention to these sins. When this happens, however, Jesus said, "Rejoice and be glad, for your reward is great in heaven . . ." (v. 12).

Those who are heirs of the kingdom are to live in accordance with God's righteousness and justice. "Think not that I have come to abolish the law and the prophets; I have come not to abolish them but to fulfil them. . . . For I tell you, unless your righteousness exceeds that of the scribes and Pharisees, you will never enter the kingdom of heaven" (vv. 17, 20).

There are two ways the word "righteousness" is used in the Bible. God is said to be righteous in forgiving the sins of the Old Testament saints as well as the sins of us who live in the present. In the Old Testament, God knew the animal sacrifices were merely symbols or shadows of the Cross where His righteous demands would be met through Christ's death. Christ's righteousness was credited to them so God would be justified in saving us. This is described as *imputed righteousness* by theologians. Since Christ has paid the penalty for our sins, there is nothing we can do to earn our salvation. "For by grace you have been saved, through faith; and that is not your own doing, it is the gift of God—not because of works, lest any man should boast" (Eph. 2:8, 9).

There are many who stop with these two verses and say that if a person has faith in Christ he is saved regardless of how he lives after declaring his faith. He does not have to fulfill the righteousness of the law in his life, for the penalty of his sins has been paid for completely. Not only that, some say it is impossible for us to live a righteous and just life on earth because of the old nature still within us. Thus, sin is often excused.

When Jesus said, "Unless your righteousness exceeds that of the scribes and Pharisees you will never enter the kingdom of heaven," he was talking about the way we live as a *result* of our faith in Him. Thus, there is not only an imputed righteousness but also an *imparted righteousness*, and the two go together. Not only did Christ pay for our sins, but He brought us into union with Him. When we were saved from the penalty of sin, we were also saved from the power of sin. This is why Paul went on to write Ephesians 2:10: "For we are his workmanship, created in Christ Jesus for good works, which God prepared beforehand, that we should walk in them." Too often, in our zeal to maintain justification by faith (which is crucial), we forget to preach the results of faith.

If I were in my thirties, I would want to be sure I was preaching a belief that behaves. I would not for a moment neglect salvation by faith through grace, for that doctrine is pivotal to our whole relationship with Jesus Christ. But I would not stop there! I would press on to the practice of obedience under the lordship of Jesus Christ.

Paul wrote, "If you confess with your lips that Jesus is Lord and believe in your heart that God raised him from the dead, you will be saved" (Rom. 10:9). This is the good news of the kingdom. Those who acknowledge that Jesus is Lord in every aspect of their lives and in all of their social, economic, and political relationships will be saved. Those who continue to live in conformity to the world and under the control of the flesh and the devil are not saved. They are not among the elect who will receive eternal life and enter into the joy of the eternal kingdom.

Christians are to serve as salt in a decaying world. Just as salt penetrates food and preserves it, we as disciples are to penetrate the world and preserve it from corruption, injustice, and unrighteousness. Jesus also calls us to be the light of the world. "Let your light so shine before men," He said, "that they may see your good works and give glory to your Father who is in heaven" (Matt. 5:16).

Too long have we had the attitude that says, "What's the use? I know I'm saved. Besides, the world is going to hell anyway. So why should I be concerned with how things are going?"

Such talk is apostasy! In fact, it was that kind of world-view that cost Israel its blessing, for God had promised His people in the Old Testament, "Now therefore, if you will obey my voice and keep my covenant, you shall be my own possession among all peoples; for all the earth is mine, and you shall be to me a kingdom of priests and a holy nation . . ." (Exod. 19:5, 6).

But they broke that covenant which God made with them. So He said, "The kingdom of God will be taken from you and given to a nation producing the fruits of it" (Matt. 22:43).

The apostle Peter does not leave us in doubt concerning the identity of the new nation that will bring forth the fruits of the kingdom. He was writing to those who have been ransomed by the blood of Christ and who have purified their souls by obedience to the truth when he said, "You are a chosen race, a royal priesthood, a holy nation, God's own people, that you may declare the wonderful deeds of him who called you out of darkness into his marvelous light" (1 Pet. 2:9).

Not only does the gospel of the kingdom provide us with hope for the future, but also it gives meaning and purpose to our lives in the present. Through Christ we have the power to live righteously and a reason to do so. Our identity as God's people provides us with a mission: the living and preaching of the gospel as a witness to all the world until the end of the age.

5

The Church Can Change Society

Dr. Karl Menninger was giving a series of lectures at Princeton Theological Seminary in 1967 when he discovered that many of those who were preparing for the ministry within the church were changing their minds. They were leaving the seminary to seek secular employment. They were convinced of the need for radical change in the social, economic, and political structures of society, but they saw the church as a part of the problem rather than as an agent of change. Religious institutions had become so much a part of the culture that they could no longer serve as correctives within it. The church itself had become too resistant to change. Young seminarians were concluding that the most effective way to change the secular structures of society was by working within them. What they did not realize was that they would encounter the same kind of people in control of the secular organizations that were resisting change within the church.

Menninger was disturbed by his discovery. As a result, he wrote a book entitled *Whatever Became of Sin?*[1] I was shocked to discover one of America's most prominent psychiatrists describing the problems of society as sin.

He admitted that he and his colleagues had been convinced that there was no such thing as sin, only various sicknesses. But the doctors found they could not heal these ills. Then, he said, some called it crime, but the officers of the law could not deal with it partly because they suffer from the "sickness" of prejudice and partiality.

Menninger came to the conclusion that we can only solve society's problems through the church. It is the one place, he said, where we can reach a cross-section of the population and appeal to the corporate conscience in an impartial way from the pulpit. However, there are many young people with high ideals who are still skeptical. They see too many problems and imperfections in the church and so they have given up on it as an agent of change.

If I were in my thirties, the first thing I would do would be to admit the weaknesses and imperfections that exist within the churches of America. I would make a list of them. Then I would search the Scriptures to find similar situations and seek to determine how they were handled by the apostles.

I have heard a lot of talk among young people about new forms of worship and getting back to the simplicity and perfection of the New Testament church. However, I am not sure what they mean by that. I recently had the privilege of speaking to a seminary graduating class. I asked them which of the New Testament churches they

[1] Karl Menninger, *Whatever Became of Sin?* (New York: Hawthorne Books, 1973).

would choose to pastor. Would they want to receive a call to pastor a church like the one Paul wrote to in Corinth? It was seriously divided. There were those within the church guilty of sexual immorality and there were some who denied the resurrection of Jesus Christ. "Perhaps," I said, "you would like to minister to a church like the one in Philippi, which was divided by a dispute between two of the leading women. Of course, there are others like Thyatira and Laodicea."

The New Testament churches were not perfect—far from it. Nor has there ever been a perfect church. Therefore, we should be realistic in our expectations. Will Rogers once said, "The good old days no longer exist and they never did." The same can be said of the church. Perfect churches no longer exist, for they never did.

One lesson you should learn from the past is to be realistic about the church and the other institutions of society as well. The disillusionment of the late sixties was the result of the failure of science, technology, and education to live up to the high expectations placed on them. You must learn to accept the church as it is with all of its flaws and imperfections, and yet never cease trying to correct them.

One reason for the failure of many churches is the lack of love for, patience with, and understanding of those within the church who resist biblically directed change by those who know such change is necessary. You may feel that as Christians they should know better. Your first impulse might be to condemn rather than to instruct them in a spirit of meekness, realizing that you also have your faults and imperfections. (Those who would be effective in the role of prophet should first serve as pastor.) You must let people know that you accept them as persons even when you cannot approve of what they may say or do.

Study the Bible so that you can provide a biblical basis for what you want to do, especially if it could be associated in the minds of people with false doctrine or improper conduct. You may know that what you propose is in accord with sound doctrine and practice, but do the other members of the church know it? Have they had the same opportunity for study and reflection, or are they acquainted with the same people who have been influential in your life? Remember, we have been called to be ambassadors of reconciliation. As such, we are to endeavor to reconcile the conflicting ideas and personalities within the church to God and to each other. We have a ministry to each other as well as to those outside the church.

In every church there is a power structure. Find out where it is and how it operates. Sometimes there are those who are competing with each other for the chief place or places within the structure. Help them by word and example to see that he who is greatest in the kingdom of God is the servant of all. We should all consider others better than ourselves; there is no place for selfish pride or personal ambition within the church. Such attitudes are in conflict with the very nature of the church and its witness to the world.

Use personal times of fellowship with your Christian brothers and sisters to help cultivate the love and compassion of Christ within them. Then they can begin to share His concern for those who are lost or alienated from God, from society, and from themselves. Share with others what God's Word teaches about our attitude toward people who are different from ourselves or who are in need of financial help.

Avoid the fads that make a game out of church. Do not try to introduce every gimmick or technique borrowed from secular education or pop psychology. Avoid sanctified therapy sessions and other substitutes for the preaching of the gospel and for calling people to repentance and confession of their sins.

Do what you can to bring spiritual warmth and vitality to the worship experience or the fellowship hour. Try to keep the services from becoming cold, formal, and ritualistic, all of which are indications of an absence of the dynamic power of the Holy Spirit. At the same time, everything should be done decently and in order.

While the focus of the church should be on the Savior, do not forget that the gospel relates to the experience of God's people. Therefore, be very sensitive to the changes that take place in society and how these changes affect the lives of people. Then find Scripture that speaks to the experiences brought about by such changes and that provides the way the church is to respond. Be aware of societal trends and learn to detect those that can be projected into the future. This will enable you to prepare yourself and those whom you influence to make the proper adjustments and to warn of impending problems to which the church should speak a prophetic word.

Remember, the people you meet and influence in church serve in various vocations and are themselves influential in the lives of others and within the corporate structures of society. If you and they are making decisions in accordance with and motivated by biblical principles, needed changes and fewer immoral acts will, in time, result. The accumulation of moral decisions and actions can make a difference in society.

If you accomplish most of these objectives, you will have a spiritual church that will attract people from your community. Success will bring with it the temptation to be proud and the feeling that God has blessed your church because of some special merit He has found in you and other members of the fellowship. Be on your guard against this. Stand up for your convictions—even those that are distinctive—but recognize that your church is only a small part of the universal church. We are to recognize our unity with all who profess to believe the gospel, who submit to the lordship of Jesus Christ, and who seek to obey His commandments. In humility, learn to repent of your own sins.

Jesus prayed that His disciples would be one even as

He and the Father are one. Our unity in Christ is to be a visible unity that Christ can use as a witness to the world, and therefore the task of each church member is to preserve the unity of Christ's body. In the same manner as the apostles, we must seek to avoid doctrinal heresy or sexual immorality from becoming a part of the church. Just as Paul instructed the church of Corinth, we are to separate ourselves from any brother or sister who teaches error or walks disorderly. But we must do so in love and with the hope of having the offending person repent, confess his sins, and be restored to fellowship in the church. "If a man is overtaken in any trespass, you who are spiritual should restore him in a spirit of gentleness" (Gal. 6:1).

Paul told the Ephesians they should "lead a life worthy of the calling . . . with all lowliness and meekness, with patience, forbearing one another in love, eager to maintain the unity of the Spirit in the bond of peace. There is one body, and one Spirit, just as you were called to the one hope . . . one Lord, one faith, one baptism, one God and Father of us all, who is above all and through all and in all" (Eph. 4:1–6).

Paul went on to say that some were given gifts "for the equipment of the saints for the work of the ministry, for building up the body of Christ, until we all attain to the *unity* of the faith and of the knowledge of the Son of God, to mature manhood, to the measure of the stature of the fullness of Christ . . . speaking the truth in love, we are to grow up in every way into him who is the head, into Christ" (Eph. 4:11–13, italics mine).

Those who have been given the gifts of apostles, prophets, evangelists, and pastors and teachers have been equipped by God to build up the body of Christ until we all attain to the *unity* of the faith. We as evangelicals have been so busy defending and proclaiming the gospel that we have overlooked one of the major goals of ministers and that is to promote *unity* within the body of Christ.

Today we measure a church's success by the size of the membership, and although growth is important, we must not compromise the gospel for the sake of numbers. We also measure success by the buildings we erect. The more expensive and elaborate the structure, the more successful we are considered to be. There is nothing wrong in having a modern and adequate building, but if it becomes a source of pride, or if money that could be used in better ways is spent on luxury and status symbols, it would be better to have no building. Most important are the spiritual goals laid out for us in the New Testament and of paramount importance is spiritual unity.

Spiritual unity should not be confused with organizational unity, which can also be a source of pride. We should never let loyalty to our particular organization interfere with our unity and fellowship with other believers within the body of Christ. We should not let our personal ambitions cause us to erect barriers between the members of the particular fellowship to which we belong and those who assemble in a different place or under a different name. Jesus Christ is Lord of the whole church—not just a particular one to the exclusion of others.

Attempts to promote spiritual unity through denominational organization have failed. Such efforts often result in the creation of other denominations that become just as sectarian as those denominations they sought to replace—and sometimes more so. We need spiritual unity that manifests itself in love for our brothers and sisters in Christ. We do not need more or larger organizations. However, the unity must be real and visible so that the world will know we are Christians. "By this all men will know that you are my disciples," said Jesus, "if you have love for one another" (John 13:35). Jesus prayed for the unity of believers knowing that through this the world would know that God had sent Him and that some might believe.

In our attempt to establish unity within the church, several issues create conflict. These must be dealt with carefully, prayerfully, patiently, and lovingly. Let's briefly consider three of these.

Conservative vs. Liberal

Many in the church today equate conservative theology with conservative politics. Dr. Chester Tulga, a very controversial preacher involved in the fundamentalist-modernist controversy, once said to me, "The average fundamentalist gets his theology from the Bible and his politics from the *Chicago Tribune*." (The *Tribune* used to be a right-wing Republican newspaper but has since modified its position.) It could also be said that the average liberal theologian gets his theology from current philosophical teaching and his politics from newspapers like *The Washington Post*.

The liberal, however, does appeal to the social and ethical teachings of Scripture to support his theological and ethical doctrines. It requires love, patience, and a knowledge of Scripture to convince the average conservative evangelical that the social and economic righteousness taught in Scripture is relevant for today. The same qualifications are required to convince the extreme liberal that individuals who control the institutions of society must be born again if they are to become more righteous and just in the production and distribution of material things.

Praise

There is a huge gap between the kinds of worship services desired by different classes and ages of people who find themselves together in one church body. There are the educated, sophisticated young adults who graduated from college in the fifties. They came to despise the emotionalism and lack of quiet atmosphere in the fundamentalist churches they outgrew. They have an appreciation for Bach and Beethoven. They like to sing the old classical hymns written by Martin Luther and John and Charles Wesley.

Some of us with less sophistication and without an ear trained for classical music still prefer the hymns of Fannie Crosby and the old gospel songs with more sentiment than theological content. "The Old Rugged Cross," "Amazing Grace," and "Tell Me the Old, Old Story" are some of the favorites.

Finally, there are the teen-agers who want to have folk music serve as an expression of their own spiritual experiences. Contemporary Christian musicians are meeting this demand.

It is snobbery of the worst kind to speak disparagingly of these tastes. After all, some of us did not have the advantage of going to schools where appreciation for classical art and music was taught. It will take some doing to satisfy all of our tastes, but it can be done. It is also possible for us to learn to appreciate each other's tastes. Both young and old can enjoy singing "Amazing Grace" as well as some of the modern folk music, which is not too unlike the old gospel tunes.

Preaching

Another point of conflict within churches focuses on the relative importance of preaching versus drama, body-life meetings, sanctified encounter groups, and dialogue and discussion groups. I enjoy dialogue and discussion but these should not become a substitute for the preaching of the Word.

The problem is that not many can do a good job in the

pulpit today. Therefore, sermons are dull and boring. More emphasis should be placed on homiletics and speech in seminaries. I predict that within the next few years preaching will regain its former status and become the chief means of arousing the conscience of congregations concerning their responsibility to society.

There are a number of other matters facing us. One of the most divisive issues with which the church is dealing is the role of women in the church—especially as it relates to the ministry.

Another area of conflict is the matter of divorce and remarriage and that of dealing with couples who live together without a legal ceremony. Unless we handle these issues lovingly but firmly, they could bring about the destruction of the moral base of our society.

All of these issues and more will necessitate our becoming skillful as ambassadors of reconciliation both within the church and without.

6

Scripture and Social Concern

"The Bible says" is a phrase often used by Billy Graham. On one occasion a person who introduced him reportedly said, "I wish Billy would tell us what Jesus says rather than what the Bible says. Jesus is our authority and not the Bible," he argued. When Dr. Graham arose to speak he said, "The only book that records the teachings of Jesus is the Bible. I therefore ask you to turn with me to that Book and we will read what Jesus says."

It is true that Jesus Christ is the head of the church and ruler over God's kingdom. Therefore, He is our authority. It is from His teaching that we receive our instructions concerning what we should believe and how we should live. However, it is also true that the only place where these instructions are recorded is in the Bible.

Not only do we find the teachings of Jesus in the Bible, but we find teachings about Him there as well. It was written by His disciples, most of whom were with Him during His earthly ministry. They wrote about the

56 IF I WERE IN MY THIRTIES

things they had learned from Him. Jesus had said that after His departure He would send the Holy Spirit who would bring all things to their remembrance. "No prophecy ever came by the impulse of man, but men moved by the Holy Spirit spoke from God" (2 Pet. 1:21).

Just as He had been sent by His Father, so Jesus sent His disciples to continue the ministry He had begun in the world. The apostle John said, "That which was from the beginning . . . which we have seen and heard we proclaim also to you, so that you may have fellowship with us; and our fellowship is with the Father and with his Son Jesus Christ" (1 John 1:1, 3). And Peter said, "You should remember the predictions of the holy prophets and the commandments of the Lord and Savior through your apostles" (2 Pet. 3:2).

The apostles were men chosen by our Lord to write the things they had seen and heard while they were with Him. They were also inspired by the Holy Spirit to teach those who heard and believed their witness. The gospel is not just the story of a historic religious leader; it is the news of One who arose from the grave. Because He lives we also live. It is the power of His resurrected life in us that enables us to live a life of obedience to His commandments.

The apostle Paul told Timothy, ". . . the sacred writings . . . are able to instruct you for salvation through faith in Jesus Christ. All scripture is inspired by God and profitable for teaching, for reproof, for correction, and for training in righteousness, that the man of God may be complete, equipped for every good work" (2 Tim. 3:15–17). Paul, of course, referred to the sacred writings of the Old Testament when he wrote this, for the New Testament Canon was not yet complete. He told Timothy that the Old Testament Scriptures were able to instruct him not only in salvation through faith in Christ Jesus, but also in righteous living.

The Law God gave Israel through Moses included

practical instructions for living righteously. An income tax on all produce was to provide for the needs of the poor. God made it clear that those who were blessed with wealth should lend without interest to their brothers who were poor. They were told not to oppress their neighbors. The wages of a hired servant were to be paid promptly, not even being held overnight. "You shall do no injustice in judgment; you shall not be partial to the poor or defer to the great, but in righteousness shall you judge your neighbor. . . . You shall love your neighbor as yourself: I am the Lord" (see Lev. 19:9, 10, 13, 15, 18).

God is not only the God of Israel, but He is also the Lord our God today. He is the same yesterday, today, and forever. Therefore, He makes the same demands upon us as He did upon Israel in regard to personal holiness, righteousness, and social and economic justice.

The Old Testament prophets told how Israel disobeyed the commandments they had promised to keep. They gleaned the entire harvest and did not leave a portion for the poor. They failed to pay a just wage to those who served them. They received favored treatment from government officials through the payment of bribes (Isa. 1:23; 3:14–15).

Isaiah condemned wives who enjoyed expensive clothes, jewelry, and perfume at the expense of laborers who were exploited by their husbands. God said the women would be brought to poverty and shame and their husbands would be killed in battle (Isa. 3:16–26).

The prophets also promised that God would send a Redeemer who would forgive the sins of those who repented and would cleanse them from their guilt (Isa. 53:1–6). Jesus was born in fulfillment of that promise. He died upon the cross not only for the sins of Israel, but for the sins of the whole world. Not only did He die, but He arose again and is now seated at the right hand of the

Father where He rules over His kingdom. The Bible tells us about the salvation He has provided for those who by faith will submit to Him as Lord and King and who will therefore live a life of righteousness and justice through the power of the Holy Spirit.

We are God's holy nation and are to obey God's commandments in regard to justice and righteousness. We not only have the forgiveness of Christ for our past sins, but we also have the indwelling presence of the Holy Spirit who gives us the power to live in accordance with His righteousness and justice in the present. We have the Scriptures of the Old Testament as well as the writings of the apostles in the New Testament from which we receive our instructions on how to live and what God expects of His chosen people. We have all of this "that the man of God may be complete, equipped for every good work" (2 Tim. 3:17).

I am puzzled by those who argue for a high view of Scripture and at the same time take a strong stand against some of us who are fighting for social and economic justice and righteousness, which according to the apostle Paul is one reason God gave us the Bible. Why is it so important for us to believe the Bible to be inspired if we are going to write articles and books defending those who do not obey its teaching and who do not subject themselves to its correction?

"Come now, and let us reason together, says the Lord: though your sins are like scarlet, they shall be as white as snow; though they are red like crimson, they shall become like wool" (Isa. 1:18). This no doubt refers to the atoning sacrifice Christ made for our sins on the cross. Just prior to this verse, Isaiah said, "Cease to do evil, learn to do good; seek justice, correct oppression" (Isa. 1: 16, 17).

In his first letter to Timothy, Paul wrote, "As for the rich in this world, charge them not to be haughty, nor to set their hopes on uncertain riches but on the living God who richly furnishes us with everything to enjoy. They are to do good, to be rich in good deeds, liberal, and generous, . . . that they may take hold of the life which is life indeed" (1 Tim. 6:17–19).

Paul did not say that it was wrong for us to have riches. In fact, he declares, they are given to us by God to enjoy. But we are not to let them take first place in our lives. "Seek first his [God's] kingdom and his righteousness," said Jesus, "and all these things shall be yours as well" (Matt. 6:33). It is a matter of priority.

Israel's sin in this regard is illustrated by the adulterous wife of Hosea: " 'She said, "I will go after my lovers, who give me my bread and my water, my wool and my flax, my oil and my drink. . . ." And she did not know that it was I who gave her the grain, the wine, and the oil, and who lavished upon her silver and gold which they used for Ba'al. . . . She . . . decked herself with her ring and jewelry, and went after her lovers, and forgot me,' says the Lord" (Hos. 2:5, 8, 13).

Israel still went through the ritual of worship. They professed to be the people of God, but they failed to obey His commandments in regard to justice and righteousness. They no longer provided for the poor and the oppressed. It was not their wealth that caused God to judge them, but the way they exploited and neglected the poor. God said He would put an end to all their holy days and appointed feasts which had become an hypocrisy because of the people's disobedience.

So it is with the gospel of "easy believism" that is being preached by many evangelicals today. There are those who boast of their wealth and who are faithful in their church attendance but become angry when any mention is made concerning their responsibility to the poor.

As I write this, I have before me an article from *Time* magazine concerning an attorney from Houston, Texas, who was elected to serve on the Supreme Court of that state. After the primary this man, who claimed to be a born-again Christian and who was a former counsel to a Christian campus organization, announced that God had instructed him to run for public office and would assist him in judicial decision-making. Only then was it revealed that some thirteen suits for bad debts and business fraud were pending against him in various courts. A former business partner claimed that he had even discussed assassinating other partners who were talking to the police.[1]

How can a man make a Christian profession, sit on the board of a Christian organization, and still live a life contrary to the righteousness and justice taught by Jesus Christ? There are many like him who see no relationship between the way they conduct their businesses or professions and their claims to being born-again Christians.

Much of the blame for this dichotomy is the result of an inadequate presentation of the gospel of Jesus Christ. When we tell a person he can accept Jesus as Savior without first explaining the need for repentance and confession, we are not telling him the whole truth. We are only presenting a partial gospel and those of us who do this in order to build up impressive statistics are false prophets who give a false message to their converts. Jesus told the Pharisees that each convert to Pharisaism was two-fold more the child of hell than he was before. Although we may not be preaching legalism, anyone who preaches a gospel that subtracts from or adds to the true gospel is as guilty of false teaching as the Pharisees were.

The Bible is uniquely and divinely inspired. Holy men of God spoke as they were carried along by the Holy Ghost. "*All* Scripture is inspired by God [God-breathed] and profitable for teaching, for reproof, for correction, for training in righteousness, that the man of God may

[1]"The Sins of Justice Yarborough," *Time*, July 18, 1977, p. 66.

be complete, equipped for every good work" (2 Tim. 3:6, italics mine).

Scriptural Authority

Once I was discussing a particular doctrine with some friends and I pointed out to them the lack of evidence for this teaching in the Bible. First, I referred to the teaching of Jesus which, if taken literally, opposes this doctrine; then I turned to one of Paul's Epistles pointing out where he also said just the opposite.

One friend, a professor who teaches systematic theology in an evangelical seminary that requires its professors to uphold the doctrine in question, admitted this to be true. "However," he said, "you are too literal in your interpretation of Scripture. You must build your system of theology first and then interpret Scripture to fit in with that system."

I replied, "If that is true, then I can build any system of theology I desire and interpret any Scripture to fit into that system."

He agreed.

Then I said that would leave us without an objective revelation to which we can appeal and whatever the Bible says to me becomes the Word of God.

Again, he agreed.

Most evangelicals would be neither as honest as my friend, nor as sincere in seeking to understand the revelation of God. Another friend who had joined in this discussion wrote me recently, reminding me of the good fellowship we had enjoyed as we discussed our views in regard to this important subject. I respect and love these men very much and I appreciate their sincerity and Christian candor. Although they could not produce Scripture for what they believed to be a fundamental doctrine of the Christian faith, they could not bring themselves to give it up.

There are many evangelicals who still hold to that which they were taught in Sunday school, church, home, or seminary, refusing to examine what they believe in the light of God's Word. These same evangelicals will take a strong stand against extreme liberals when they deny certain portions of the Bible that do not fit their scientific or philosophical system.

Both liberals and evangelicals will quote from the portions of the Bible that seem to support their positions. Both sides are sometimes guilty of twisting the meaning of Scripture and making it say something the writer never intended. Quite often we formulate theological systems (or adopt one formulated by our favorite theologian) and then we go to the Bible to pick and choose those verses that fit our system and leave the rest, including those that would disprove some points of the system. In this way we treat the Bible much the same as we choose our food from a smorgasbord table at a restaurant. We pick what we want to eat and leave the rest.

When I was a young pastor, I began to realize that I was guilty of not letting God speak to me through His Word. Rather, I was seeking to prove my own beliefs by using the Bible in an arbitrary manner.

I then laid aside my reference Bible and purchased one without notes. I adopted a very simple method of study which I have found very helpful ever since. Instead of going to the Bible with presuppositions I want to prove, I seek to lay these aside and free my mind as much as possible from all preconceived ideas and biases I may have. (Of course, none of us can do this completely because the way we think or interpret certain words or sentences is determined by all that has influenced and shaped us since birth. But we must try to recognize what our presuppositions are and bring them under the judgment and correction of the Word of God.)

Then I choose a particular Book or Letter from the Sacred Canon. After reading it through several times so that I can close the Book and think my way through it, I go back and read it more carefully, seeking answers to the following questions:

1. Author: Who is the human author of the Book?
2. Addressee: To whom was it written?
3. Purpose: Why did he write it?
4. Message: In the light of his purpose, what did he say? Was he trying to prove something? If so, what and why? What arguments did he give?
5. Application: Is there a principle that can be derived from the Book that can be applied to a similar concern or situation today? Are there any illustrations from modern life to which this message would apply?

Instead of trying to make the Scriptures harmonize with the philosophy of men, I seek to draw from the Bible that which will reveal the Lord Jesus Christ and how we are to relate to Him and His kingdom today. Martin Luther, John Calvin, and the other reformers found in the Bible the answers to the problems they encountered in what they believed to be an apostate church. John Wesley was able to find what was needed in his day, and so it was with Jonathan Edwards and Charles Finney in their particular situations.

We are living in an age of crisis and change similar to that of the Reformation and the colonial revivals. We should follow the examples of these saints of the past and study the Word of God for ourselves in the light of our contemporary situation. Perhaps the Lord will speak to us as He did to them. Perhaps we also can speak a prophetic word from God to our generation.

7

The Christian Ethic

One of the most popular and articulate spokesmen for fundamentalism was the silver-tongued orator William Jennings Bryan. He is best known for his defense of the biblical account of creation in the attempt to keep the theory of evolution from being taught in the schools of Tennessee. The Scopes trial brought him into conflict with the brilliant and famous lawyer Clarence Darrow. The liberal press and the modernist theologians were on the side of Darrow, but the average person was in sympathy with Bryan. Even to this day the accounts of the trial declare Darrow the winner even though the court decision favored Bryan's position.

Bryan was the Democratic candidate for president of the United States in three elections, but each time he lost to his Republican opponent. However, he became secretary of state under President Woodrow Wilson. While in that position, he was severely criticized by his colleagues and the press for his opposition to the proposal that Dr. Charles Eliot, former president of Harvard University, be appointed as ambassador to China. Eliot was a Unitarian and Bryan thought that his views against biblical Christianity would be detrimental to the ministry of the missionaries who had labored so long and sacrificially in bringing the gospel to China. He was also criticized for his refusal to serve liquor at the State Department receptions and dinners.

These issues that characterize Bryan as a fundamentalist are well known, but his strong stand for social and economic righteousness has largely been ignored. Social concern was a part of historic fundamentalism, in continuation of the evangelical emphasis that grew out of the colonial revivals.

Bryan was against organic evolution because its proponents sought to use it to discredit the Genesis account of creation, but he was also against social Darwinism because it placed black people at the bottom of the evolutionary ladder and white Anglo-Saxons at the top. He was against economic Darwinism which was based upon the evolutionary hypothesis of the "survival of the fittest." This, he felt, justified the worst and most corrupt forms of capitalism characterized by rat-race or cut-throat, dog-eat-dog competition.

Bryan was a Populist who believed in the rights of the laboring class. He opposed what he believed to be the exploitation of workers by the Rockefellers, Morgans, and other multimillionaires. He saw the common man as one who worked long hours at barely subsistence wages to produce the wealth that was being accumulated by a few families and passed on to their heirs. On one occasion when an article appeared in a newspaper about Rockefeller teaching a Bible class, Bryan said, "I do not see how one man can do so much preaching and practice so much sinning."[1]

He took a strong stand against illegal profiteering dur-

[1]George Dollar, *The History of Fundamentalism* (Greenville, S.C.: Bob Jones University, 1973).

ing World War I and proposed to the Presbyterian General Assembly a motion that would require all those guilty of profiteering to be expelled from their churches. He warned that "it would be embarrassing to someday have a sheriff enter a prominent church, take a prominent person from a prominent pew and charge him with stealing from the rest of the congregation." He argued, "We do not need a Presbyterian ward in the profiteers prison."[2]

Bryan was in favor of an eight-hour day (when men were forced to work twelve and fourteen hours a day), old-age pensions, guaranteed bank deposits, and other social and economic reforms.

He was a true evangelical in that he believed in an individual conversion experience as the only means to a life of purity and social righteousness. Later, fundamentalists dropped the need for social righteousness from their messages, and there are some today who are eliminating the necessity for a life of holiness. The next step could be the elimination of the need for a conversion experience. When this happens we will be at the same place establishment churches were prior to the revivals that caused the phenomenal growth and influence of the evangelical churches during the first century of our existence as a nation.

Bryan warned the churches not to accept the tainted money of the multimillionaires who were exploiting the people working for them in order to build up their massive fortunes. The churches did not take his advice and with very few exceptions major evangelists from D. L. Moody to the present ones have been financed by the people whom Bryan condemned. In return, evangelical pulpits have been silenced on the economic evils that are condemned so strongly by Jesus, the prophets, and the apostles. In fact, many right-wing fundamentalists equate the gospel with right-wing politics and the interests of the rich and powerful.

Not all rich men are exploiting workers, consumers, or the public. Some of the finest people I know are extremely wealthy, but they are using their money and the power it brings them as God directs. The sons and daughters of some of the families condemned by Bryan have recognized that the way their inherited wealth was accumulated was wrong; some have suffered a deep sense of guilt because of it. Some of the most liberal programs advocated by Bryan to help the common man have been sponsored by men like Franklin D. Roosevelt, Jr., Nelson Rockefeller, Jr., and John and Edward Kennedy.

When President Roosevelt took office, I was working in the mail department of a bank from 1:00 A.M. until 9:00 A.M. six days a week and attending high school in the daytime. My salary was forty-five dollars per month. Sometimes I had to work all day Saturday and Sunday without extra pay. When Roosevelt took office, he established regulations requiring overtime pay for more than forty-four hours of work per week. His administration also established a minimum-wage law which immediately raised my salary to sixty-five dollars a month. You can't imagine what a help that was for my family.

My father was a bricklayer making forty-five cents an hour. It was during the Depression and he worked only one or two days a week. We sometimes went for weeks without having meat on the table or enough clothes to wear. I still feel I am living in luxury because I can put on fresh clothes every day and need my laundry washed only once a week. What a contrast this is with having only two shirts and two pairs of socks.

I thank God for the increased sense of security for retired people now that there is social security and medical care. These were things that were championed by historic evangelicals and their fundamentalist successors before they began to accept what Bryan called "the tainted money of the rich." Now it is the sons and daughters of the rich who are for social justice, and the opposition comes from modern evangelicals. If not open opposition, there is at least a noticable silence in many pulpits on this aspect of the gospel.

Those in the upper levels of business management are beginning to realize that they have a responsibility for improving the social and economic conditions of our society. I belong to a book club for business executives and there appears to be an increasing awareness of the responsibility corporate managers have toward employees and consumers as well as toward stockholders.

I have in my hand a book entitled *The Struggle for Identity* by Roger M. D'Aprix. The author says,

Our companies are very much like the rest of our institutions. The old dogma is being questioned and discredited but very little is being done to articulate a new view of what the institution is and what it must become. Currently we are somewhere in a position between the old and the new. It is a painful and confusing transitional period for both management and individual employees.

During the next few years while the new dogma is being formulated, the individual employee must fend for himself in deciding what his relationship will be with his organization. The individual in our contemporary companies must search for a workable philosophy that will sustain him during the transitional period.

If he clings to the old company dogma, he runs the risk of living a life in which his company values will ultimately put him in severe conflict with his society. Conversely, if he embraces the new value system too enthusiastically and tries to implement it in his company environment, he will quickly find himself in conflict with the old values of profit and growth. In the old style company there will be a tendency to resist these values as subversive and extremely dangerous, and therefore, the individual trauma will be greater for those who no longer subscribe to the old dogma. So the answer in my opinion is to adopt a suitable personal perspective at least for this transitional period.[3]

This is good advice not only for young executives in business corporations, but also for young executives in denominations and for pastors of churches that are resistant to the necessary changes that must be made if we are to survive the present crisis created by the social, economic, ethical, and environmental problems of our society. The quotation I have given is just one of many that could be gleaned from books written for businessmen today showing the business community's growing awareness of its responsibilities to society as well as to its stockholders' and its members' own financial interests.

Dr. Daniel Bell, a professor of sociology at Harvard University, has written a book entitled *The Cultural Contradictions of Capitalism.* He contends that capitalism is destroying the culture that produced it.

That culture, declares Bell, was built upon the Protestant ethic of faith in God, work as a sacred calling, honesty, and frugality. Those who have produced the science and technology that has been so beneficial to capitalism have also done their best to destroy religious faith. They created a new life-style in order to maintain an expanding market for its goods and services.

For thousands of years the function of economics was to provide the daily necessities—the subsistence of life. For various upper-class groups, it has been the basis of status and a sumptuous style. But now on a mass scale, economics has become geared to the demands of culture. Here too, culture, not as expressive symbolism or moral meanings but as life-style, came to reign supreme.

[3]Roger D'Aprix, *The Struggle for Identity* (New York: Dow Jones-Irwin, Inc., 1972), pp. 20–30.

The new capitalism continued to demand a Protestant ethic in the area of production (that is, in the realm of work), but it also stimulated a demand for pleasure and play in the matter of consumption. Bell goes into great detail to describe how the capitalist promotes instant self-gratification in order to market his products and services. "One is to be 'straight' [ie. practice the work ethic] by day," he says, "and a 'swinger' by night."[4]

It seems strange to me that some of the most incisive statements being made about the decadence of modern culture and the materialism and hedonism of our society are not coming from evangelical pulpits, but from professors in secular universities. Too many Christians who, like myself, came out of a life of poverty are now so comfortable in their affluent environment that they do not want to remember their past. They do not want their consciences troubled by those who for various reasons were not able to escape their poverty-stricken environment.

This is a highly emotional issue among evangelicals and we have to tread softly as we talk about it. But talk about it we must, for we are in the midst of a sociological and economic problem that demands a spiritual solution. Scientists and social engineers have tried all their theories but have experienced little success. As a result, when we approach the average college student or man on the street today, we encounter a spirit of apathy and cynicism.

The encouraging side of the picture is the admission of failure by liberals in the academic community and the recognition that we must get back to our biblical roots if we are to find a solution.[5] Christians are becoming

[4]Daniel Bell, *The Cultural Contradictions of Capitalism* (New York: Basic Books, 1976), p. 70.

[5]Some of the leading intellectuals today such as Robert Bellah, Daniel Bell, and Leonard Silk are saying that we should get back to a biblical ethic. There are also people who are writing for business executives who are emphasizing the need for social and corporate morality on the part of business corporations.

aware of our social problems and seeking biblical answers. This is very different from the way it was when I was in my thirties. All we could think about was getting a good education, a well-paying job, a home in the suburbs, a new and expensive car, fine clothes, and the right people to help us climb the social and economic ladder of success.

This is not to say that these are not still the motives of the average person. This attitude has returned to the campus and has become very evident in the competition that exists for grades and recognition. Such motivation, I believe, is a result of the failure of social experiments in the past and the lack of fresh new ideas of how to change things in the future. If there is no possibility of effecting significant change, then students feel they might as well get what they can, while they can, for there is no certainty they will be here tomorrow.

I look at this attitude change among college students with mingled emotions. I am glad that students are no longer rioting, locking deans in their offices, and blowing up laboratories. That is senseless and sinful violence for which there is no purpose except to give vent to pent-up emotions. However, I am concerned about their apathy regarding the problems to be encountered as they enter the business world.

If I were in my thirties today I would, of course, seek to discover God's will for my life. In doing that, I would not minimize the old Protestant ethic that saw secular vocations as a sacred calling. Young men and women should prepare themselves for secular careers with the same sense of dedication that they would have if they were preparing for ministry in the church. I would look for a place of employment where I could best use the talent the Lord had given me. I would be concerned about the interests of my employer and co-laborers and would try to be honest and open with both. I would perform my task with the single purpose of bringing glory to God.

If I should succeed to a position of management, I

would endeavor to make every decision in the light of the Christian ethic. I would try to be concerned about the quality of the product or services being offered to the public. I would want to know that advertising was honest and did not manipulate people into buying things they did not need or could not afford.

A person told me recently that he was out of work and needed employment. He was given a job selling swimming pools. He talked a young couple who were expecting a baby and barely making ends meet into buying the most expensive pool sold by his company. He knew they could not afford it. Just as they were about to sign, he suggested they save their money for the expenses they would have with the arrival of the baby. He needed that sale but not badly enough to betray his Lord and this couple. He also quit the job.

There is nothing wrong in making a good salary if we earn it honestly and without hurting or exploiting someone else in the process. There is nothing wrong in having a comfortable home and a nice car or dressing well as long as we do not have to take unfair advantage of others to obtain these things. It also becomes wrong when we become arrogant toward those who do not have them and especially toward those who are dependent upon us for their financial well-being.

I do not think Christians should refuse to work for secular corporations, but rather we should seek to penetrate them and use whatever influence we have to make them responsive to the needs of society. We should endeavor to produce that which will build up and not tear down the moral and spiritual foundation without which no culture can long endure.

If I were in my thirties and following a career in business, I would use whatever influence I could develop to stop the widespread use of bribery in order to get contracts from the government. I would try to eliminate the use of kickbacks to purchasing agents of companies using the products mine was producing. I would do my best to eliminate discrimination in employment and promotion because of a person's race, ethnic origin, or sex.

In every office there are personality conflicts and conflicts of interest. Some managers promote these because they think that competition is good for business. It may be good for business, but it is not any more ethical or moral than promoting a cock fight. A young executive should respect his superiors, but that does not mean he should always agree with their managerial methods or decisions.

There once was a man on the board of directors of the Conservative Baptist Home Mission Society who had been honest enough to let me know that he did not agree with my policies nor with my theology as it pertained to social righteousness. He sincerely believed that such theology was part of the liberal social gospel and that we should not have anything to do with that which denied the essentials of the Christian faith. I understood his concern.

When his three-year term was up, he informed me that he would not be able to accept another term if offered. I replied that we would cut down on some extra committee work we had been assigning him if he would change his mind. I then explained my reasons:

1. I needed someone whose views were different from mine to make me prove that my proposals were right and to offer corrections when I was wrong. He had the courage and the ability to do that in a gracious manner.
2. He represented a minority of people in our movement who feel as he does. We need to hear those opinions expressed on the various issues that come before us.

3. There were times when I agreed with him and others on the board didn't. He saved me from standing alone on those issues.
4. I said, and I meant it, "I like you as a person and would miss your fellowship."

He did accept another term and made a valuable contribution to the board and to my own spiritual development. Someday I hope to convince him that there is a difference between the liberal social gospel and biblical social concern. But if I fail, I will still want him as a friend and respect him for the valuable contribution he made to the board.

The same principle applies to those who serve as my co-workers on the administrative staff. They are encouraged to take issue with me when they think I am wrong. I appreciate the times when they keep me from making serious mistakes and make valuable contributions to the decisions that have to be made on important issues. We work together as a team. I appreciate the love and respect that I receive from them. I also respect their abilities and the contributions they make to the ministry of the society in which we serve together. It is exciting to work with them and I always cherish the time we spend together in the service of the Master.

The way to change the structures of society is through the dedicated leadership of individuals who are committed to the Christian ethic.

8

How Biblical Is Black Theology?

"If there is a God and if He is the Christian God, He hates black people."

These words were spoken in the midst of a discussion I had with a class in black studies at a state university. I had been asked to lecture on Christian ethics.

At the conclusion of my lecture, a black student said, "I can accept your ethic but not your God."

A discussion followed my reply, during which another black student arose and said by contrast, "I know that God loves me and I am black. He is my Lord and Savior and I enjoy precious fellowship with Him each day."

There are, of course, countless black brothers and sisters who could give similar testimonies concerning God's love for them and how they have experienced it. However, this does not remove the problem that has been caused by those who are white and have professed to be Christians while harboring prejudice in their hearts against blacks and other minorities. The charge that the Sunday morning worship service is the most segregated hour during the week is still largely true, although many churches are beginning to recognize that it is wrong. But they often do not know how to correct it.

Even more painful to blacks are the indignities and poverty they suffer as a result of the subtle, even unconscious racism that exists in white society and keeps them from finding meaningful and profitable employment. They were long barred from the labor unions of carpenters and other skilled crafts, and promotions to executive positions were typically given to whites even if blacks were more qualified. These problems are gradually being corrected, but not fast enough to relieve the suffering that millions still have to endure in the midst of an affluent society. These conditions and many others have existed during the life of this nation and except for brief periods of time have been condoned by the churches through their actions, their preaching, or their silence.

There was then some justification for the student's feeling that the God of the Christians hates black people. That is what we had demonstrated to him by attitude, word, and actions. This has caused some black theologians to reject the theology produced by whites and to produce what is called "black" or "liberation theology." This is based upon an interpretation of the Bible through their own experience of suffering the oppression of a white racist society.

There are those within the United States and in the Third World who refer to Christianity as the white man's religion. It was designed, they believe, to keep them in a place of servitude to the white Anglo-Saxon race. The way they have been exploited by the so-called Christian nations would also justify their attitude.

It is difficult to explain the difference between the

biblical gospel and the way it has been represented by those who profess to be Christians. The gospel of "easy believism" is doing more damage to the cause of evangelism than almost anything else.

I suggest we consider the arguments being made for liberation theology by the various theologians who are seeking to undo the damage of those who have falsely professed to be disciples of Jesus. These have demonstrated the kind of hatred, arrogance, greed, and prejudice which He denounced strongly and which led to His being nailed to a tree by those who did not want to have Him rule over them.

The argument of blacks and other minority groups in the United States is similar to that of theologians in Latin America and other parts of the Third World. They say that the theology of our churches is the result of an effort by Europeans and Americans of European descent to interpret Scripture to fit the notion that we Anglo-Saxons are God's chosen people and that He has destined us to rule over the rest of the world. They charge we have done this through the power of our military might, economic superiority, and colonial missionary activity.

It may be easy for us to deny this; however, anyone who makes an objective study of history will discover that both military and pioneer missionary activity were motivated by the Manifest Destiny theory. The Puritans justified the confiscation of Indian land by saying that God had chosen them to convert and civilize the heathen. Indians were murdered by soldiers who believed themselves to have a divine mandate to bring Indians into subjection.

The same argument was used to justify the slavery of black people from Africa. Some people condemned the television version of Roots because it pictured the cruelty of the white slaveholder. One critic said many slaveholders were Christians who would not have treated slaves cruelly. Such a defense, however, is totally insensitive to the cruelty of slavery itself, regardless of the physical treatment of slaves by individual masters. That some slaves were not beaten does not hide the fact that they would have been if they had tried to escape, and no person with any self-respect wants to remain as another human being's slave.

The segregation of blacks after slavery has continued into the present day. There are still many persons who claim to be Christians and yet believe in this cruel and inhuman treatment of millions of people who were created in the image and likeness of God. These so-called Christians will even misquote and distort the teaching of the Bible to justify their sin against God and their fellow men.

As a young man, I heard a pastor say from the pulpit that God had placed a curse on Ham and that he was the father of the black race. I believed that and taught it myself as a young pastor. It never occurred to me that a pastor who was a brilliant man with a Th.D. from a conservative seminary would tell me something that was not in the Bible. I am confident he had been taught the same thing when he was a boy and it never occurred to him to see if the Bible actually taught what he was saying.

I was to teach a class for Inter-Varsity Christian Fellowship on a Friday night and the passage concerning Ham was to be included in the subject for the evening. I decided I had better look it up so that I could easily turn to it if some student should ask a question. To my amazement, it was not there! I read the passage in Genesis that tells about Noah's arousing from a drunken stupor and placing a curse upon one of his sons. But it was not Ham but Canaan, the son of Ham (Gen. 9:18–27). How embarrassed I was to discover that I was about to teach something that was not in the Bible. I searched the Scripture to see if the Canaanites ever went to Africa, but I could find no place indicating they ever left the Holy Land. I turned to the history books and could not find it there either. I looked at the clock and saw that I had two hours to prepare another study!

This false teaching was invented by the pastors of slaveholders to justify the sin of their wealthy members. It did not matter that the Word of God was used to justify one of the greatest sins ever committed by a nation. It was more important from the pastor's viewpoint to keep his job in an influential and highly respected church. This lie has been repeated throughout the history of our nation and is still being taught in many fundamentalist pulpits today.

During the revivals that began with the ministry of Dr. Charles Finney, a strong stand was taken in evangelical pulpits against slavery and other social sins of that era. People by the thousands were brought under deep conviction, repented of their sinful attitudes toward blacks along with other sins, such as adultery, drunkenness, gambling, and murder. They confessed them to God and received His forgiveness and cleansing at the Cross. The Holy Spirit brought about a transformation in their lives and it was not long until these new converts began to make a tremendous impact upon society. Slavery was abolished and the Civil War followed.

After the war, the revival was over and everything returned to normal. Blacks were freed, but whites as a whole had not been freed from their prejudice. They still looked upon blacks as inferior and would not mix with them socially or in their churches. Blacks still had to be subservient to white people.

The Ku Klux Klan was organized to keep blacks in their place, that is, to see that they did not get an education and were not allowed to mix socially with white people. Even some Baptist and other evangelical preachers joined the Klan. There are still those in evangelical churches in the South who preach from their pulpits that blacks should not be allowed to integrate with whites.

In the North, we have hypocritcally condemned the

South for its segregated buses, schools, and lunch counters while maintaining segregated housing and, therefore, segregated schools (which are not kept on a par with white schools). Those blacks who, in spite of the system, managed to get a college education were not allowed to hold executive positions in industry. In large part, segregation has kept blacks poor, illiterate, underfed, and living in slums.

Not only has the biblical gospel been compromised in order to keep blacks from participating in the social life of our nation and from competing with whites economically and politically, but also the judicial system has been against them. We have very few preachers of the gospel who call attention to this sin for which our nation is now being judged.

When I was in Senegal with my wife Ruth in 1967, I went for a walk one day while our missionary host was busy. As I passed a nearby university, some of the students greeted me and we were soon engaged in a conversation that lasted for about an hour. "Why do you hate black people in the United States?" was the most important question I had to answer.

My reply was that most of our churches had not taken a Christian stand on racism and that most of the members had never really understood it as sin. If they had, they would have a different attitude toward blacks and other minorities.

Our evangelical churches are filled with people most of whom have never heard the biblical gospel applied to these issues. I told the students of some who are trying to change the situation and of the progress that has been made. However, I admitted, we still have a long way to go. The Africans became very serious as I explained the gospel to them further and one of them later came to the home of the missionary to talk further about Jesus Christ and the gospel.

The attitude that we have held toward blacks and

other minority groups is well known throughout the world. There are even missionaries who are racists and they are unable to hide it from those whom they are trying to evangelize. The African churches have become strong enough and their pastors now have enough education to read the Bible for themselves and to develop their own theology. They now want the Good News of Christ preached in their pulpits without all the European and American cultural baggage that has so long been brought with it by well-meaning missionaries. The gospel has to be relevant to the culture if it is going to serve as salt and light, but it should not be compromised or interpreted in a way that will condone that which is unjust and evil in a culture.

Christianity is said to be the white man's religion which was designed to keep the nonwhite people of the world in subjection, serving the needs of the white people and catering to their egos. This is not the true gospel, but it is believed by some missionaries to be true because it is what they were taught in their homes, churches, and seminaries. The white man's religion that distorts the biblical gospel and seeks to keep the two thirds of the world that is nonwhite in subjection to the one third that is white is not the true gospel. It is not true to Jesus Christ nor to the Bible from which we know of Christ and the doctrine He sets forth for His disciples.

Let us take a look at liberation theology. Since we are more familiar with what has happened in the United States and since what we do here affects what we do in other parts of the world, let's begin with black theology.

At a theological commission of black churchmen, a statement was drawn up of which the following is the opening paragraph:

Black people affirm their being. This affirmation is made in the whole experience of being Black in the hostile American society. Black theology is not a gift of the Christian gospel dispensed to slaves; rather it is an appropriation which Black slaves made of the gospel given by their oppressors. Black theology has been nurtured, sustained, and passed on in the Black churches in their various ways of expression. Black theology has dealt with all the ultimate and violent issues of life and death for a people despised and degraded.[1]

The warrant for black theology, then, is black oppression. Its exponents claim the religion of Israel depended upon Israel's need for deliverance from Egyptian bondage. Over and over again God reminded them that He was the one who delivered them from their oppression in Egypt.

When Jesus spoke in the synagogue of Nazareth, He read from the scroll of Isaiah: "He [the Lord] has anointed me to preach good news to the poor. He has sent me to proclaim release to the captives . . . to set at liberty those that are oppressed . . ." (Luke 4:18).

One view of black liberation theology is expressed by author James Cone who writes, "Black theology is Christian theology precisely because it has the Black predicament as its point of departure."[2] White Christians, according to Cone, must therefore become black in order to be Christians. Cone continues:

Being in America has very little to do with skin color. To be black means that your heart, your soul, your mind, and your body are where the dispossessed are. . . . Therefore, being reconciled to God does not mean that one's skin is physically black. It essentially depends on the color of your heart, soul, and mind. The focus on blackness does not mean that only

[1]Gayraud S. Welmore, Black Religion and Black Radicalism (New York: Doubleday 1973), p. 292.
[2]James Cone, A Black Theology of Liberation (Philadelphia: J. P. Lippincott Co., 1970), pp. 27–28.

blacks suffer as victims in a racist society but blackness is a symbol of what oppression means in America . . . Blackness, then, stands for all victims of oppression who realize that their humanity is inseparable from man's liberation from whiteness.[3]

There are other black scholars who take issue with Cone and say that black theology comes out of the black experience in America. It is the way blacks sing, pray, and preach. According to these scholars, black theology is a life-style that has been developed during the more than two hundred years of suffering and oppression they have endured. It is the folk religion that has grown out of their experience.

The black experience, of course, cannot be shared by a white person no matter how much sympathy he may have for the plight of black people and no matter how much persecution he may suffer for the stand he takes in their behalf. He cannot share their experience any more than a person with a blindfold can share the experience of a blind person. However we can learn from the black experience and we can seek to carry to completion the mission begun by our Lord to relieve the oppressed and release the slaves.

We may not entirely agree with Cone, but anyone who has made a serious and unbiased study of the subject will have to admit that there is far more biblical evidence for black theology than for white. One of the greatest sins of the white evangelical church is its failure to condemn the racism in our culture that has caused the suffering of millions of our citizens for no reason other than their skin pigment.

On one occasion I was speaking to a convention on the West Coast. The topic of my sermon was, "A United Church for a Divided World." I had talked about the

[3]*Ibid.*

division that exists between rich and poor, young and old, and white and nonwhite. I referred to the Scriptures that reveal the ministry of reconciliation God has given to the members of the church.

When I finished there was a time for questions, most of which centered on the division between white and nonwhite. After several questions had been answered, one lady asked if an integrated church might lead to intermarriage?

I replied that it might.

She said, "Do you think that is right?"

I replied that when any couple requests me to perform their marriage ceremony there are a number of questions I ask them to make sure they understand some of the problems they will encounter in the marriage relationship. If a couple of different racial backgrounds should approach me about marriage I would want to know if they fully understood the problems they would encounter both in the black and the white community. I would want to make sure they were getting married because they really loved each other and not to prove how liberal they were. I said, "When I have satisfied myself on these points I do not know of any biblical reason why they should not be married."

One pastor stood to his feet and said, "I have been a member of this association for seven years and in all that time I have never heard anyone make a statement like that." (I began to sink in my chair waiting for what he would say next.) Then he turned and pointed his finger at me and said, "Thank God you had the courage to say it."

The audience applauded.

There were some pastors, however, who did not like it. When we had our annual meetings, they, along with some lay persons, came prepared to see that I was not reelected to the position in which I serve. Some of them were rather angry, but they were unable to get a large enough following for ample support. Tempers cooled down before the elections and I received a favorable vote.

Prior to the elections I talked with a prominent layman who was very upset. He said, "I am going back to my church and have them cut off everything they are giving to the Society."

I said that was not only his privilege but his duty if he felt that way. I also said, "You should try to get the other delegates who are here to do the same thing. However, before you do I think you should know that it will not cause me to change my position in regard to the sin of segregation. I will continue to preach against it and to preach in favor of integration. I promised God when I took this position I would not compromise on the biblical gospel either to hold the job or to raise money for the Society."

In my stance as an evangelical I believe there are three doctrines of Scripture that are very important to the Christian faith. They are the doctrines of *Creation*, the *Cross* and the *Church*. I asked my brother to look at the Bible with me to see what it had to say on each of these doctrines.

The Creation

The Bible declares that God created man in his own image and likeness. It does not say he created *white man* in his own image but *man*. That includes the one third of the human race that is white and the two thirds that is nonwhite. To say that either one or the other is inferior is to say that God is a respector of persons. Social Darwinism teaches that man is in a process of evolving from lower to higher forms of existence. Those who hold this view teach that blacks are at the lower rung of the evolutionary ladder and white Anglo-Saxons are at the top. As a conservative evangelical I prefer to accept the Genesis account of creation and reject that of Social Darwinism.

The Cross

The Bible can quite naturally be divided into three periods of time during which three kinds or stocks of humanity have dominated the earth: (1) the Gentiles, (2) the Jews, and (3) the new humanity in Christ.

The first period of human history is recorded in Genesis 1–11. During this time there was only one kind of humanity on the earth, the Gentile who looked to Adam as the head. This period lasted for two thousand years according to Ussher's Chronology. (Most scholars believed it was much longer than that.) It is recorded in the first eleven chapters in Genesis and ends in judgment at the tower of Babel.

The second period begins with the call of Abraham in Genesis 12 and continues through the remainder of the Old Testament and into the New Testament, ending at the Cross. During this period of time we have another kind of people, the Jews, who were the descendents of Abraham. This was a two-thousand year period.

The third period began at the Cross and has lasted almost two thousand years. During this period we see another kind of people taken from the two already mentioned: the new man in Christ.

The apostle Paul was speaking of the Gentiles during the second period when he said, "Remember that at that time you were separated from Christ, alienated from the commonwealth of Israel, and strangers to the covenants of promise, having no hope and without God in the world. But now in Christ Jesus you who once were far off have been brought near in the blood of Christ. For he is our peace, who . . . has broken down the dividing wall of hostility . . . that he might create in himself one new man in place of two, so making peace, and might reconcile us both to God in one body through the cross, thereby bringing the hostility to an end" (Eph. 2:12–16).

At the Cross not only is man reconciled to God, but man is also reconciled to man. You cannot have one without the other. To deny that people from all races, tongues, and people have been brought together at the Cross is to deny that for which Jesus shed His blood. To do that is to cease to be biblical.

The Church

The third argument I presented to my friend pertains to the church. "For by one Spirit we were all baptized into one body—Jews or Greeks, slaves or free—and all were made to drink of one Spirit. . . . there may be no discord in the body, but that the members may have the same care for one another. If one member suffers, all suffer together; if one member is honored, all rejoice together" (1 Cor. 12:13, 25, 26). To deny the teaching of the inspired apostle concerning the unity of the body of Christ is to cease to be biblical or evangelical.

Before I had finished, tears were running down my friend's face. He assured me he would not follow through with his threat to have his church cut off their giving. A few weeks later we received a personal commitment of $3,000 per year over and above what his church was giving.

If I were in my thirties today I would make the same appeal for an integrated church that I have been making for the last forty years. Except, I would perhaps make it even stronger. For in Christ there is no racial or ethnic division—we are all one in Him.

9

How Biblical Is Third World Theology?

There are those in the Third World who are calling for a moratorium on missions. This call is not being issued by unbelievers. Nor is it directed toward those who belong to religions other than Christianity or to the liberal wing of Christianity.

There are evangelicals who, while believing all the fundamental doctrines of the Christian church, are saying that missionaries should go home and remain for about five years before returning. They have good reasons for making these demands and these reasons should be understood by the churches of the Western world.

The first reason can be attributed to the success of missionaries who have labored in the past. They have built churches, schools, and hospitals. The nationals have been trained and are being trained to do the work that was, by necessity, formerly done by the missionaries. Some have taken advanced training and have demonstrated that they are as gifted as the missionaries. Some are even better trained and more capable of communicating the gospel in their own language and culture than we are. Many of the mission churches are growing and prospering. They often have more spiritual vitality than the churches from which missionaries are sent. They are dedicated to Christ and aware of the spiritual needs of fellow citizens.

The story is told of a pastor from the United States who was sitting next to a pastor from the Third World. The one from the States introduced himself, gave the name of his church, and mentioned that it had fifteen thousand members. The Third World pastor gave his name and that of his church and said that it had thirty thousand members.

The national association of Baptist churches to which I belong has less than twelve hundred churches in its membership. The association of the same denomination in a South American country has twenty-five hundred churches, more than double the size of the one from which some of their missionaries come.

We need to recognize the indigenous leadership in churches of Third World countries and begin to make plans for turning the property and control of the ministry over to them. This is in keeping with the ideals of most mission boards, but in practice the turning over of responsibilities has been slow. The nationals are telling us they are ready.

The second reason for a moratorium on missions stems from cultural differences. Many missionaries from the United States subconsciously believe that our American culture is a product of the Christian gospel. Not many of them are aware of the "Manifest Destiny theory," that was advocated early in our history as an excuse for appropriating the land of the Indians. This theory also allowed for our colonial policies of exploiting the labor and natural resources of Third World countries to satisfy our own material greed as well as to justify our missionary activity. Nevertheless, many missionaries still harbor the feeling that America is a Christian nation and superior to others. Many believe we are a superior race of people.

In the early colonial times it was boldly stated that the purpose of missions was to preach the gospel and civilize the heathen. These terms are no longer used by enlightened missionaries, but the attitude still persists and the nationals can easily detect it in conduct if not in speech. Often we are unconsciously betrayed by what we say.

We have been raised in a racist culture. Even though we may accept in theory the idea that all people are created in the image and likeness of God and that Christ died on the cross in order that all might be reconciled to God and to each other, our subconscious tells us this is not so. Strange as it may seem, there are still some missionaries who will openly express racist and chauvinistic views.

I recently talked with a retired missionary who had spent her life teaching in the Far East. I was surprised at the hatred she expressed for blacks in the United States. When I asked how she as a missionary could harbor such hostility, she justified herself by saying she loved the Oriental people among whom she had worked. A little later in the conversation I mentioned that I knew missionaries who did not care enough about the people they served to learn the language. She immediately informed me that she had never learned to speak Chinese. That ended the conversation and I am afraid temporarily damaged a good friendship which I hope can be restored.

A missionary who lives with people for a long time and yet cannot communicate with them in their own language cannot adequately understand their culture and, therefore, is unable to relate the gospel to their needs.

This brings us to the third reason for criticism of missions by nationals: the harm done to the native culture by past missionaries who have condemned traditional rites and social ceremonies as pagan without first determining if they are contrary to Scripture. In many cases these so called "heathen" practices were no different than our laying a wreath on a grave, saluting the flag, or firing a volley at a military funeral.

We seem to forget that some of our own special days such as Christmas and Easter originally began as Pagan holidays and only took on Christian significance after the church was united with the state under Constantine. There is even a growing tendency to make the pagan aspects of these holidays a part of our Christian worship. Sometimes even Santa Claus and the Easter bunny are included in church programs. Why should we think of these as harmless while condemning similar practices in Third World countries?

Most missionaries now recognize our past mistakes in this regard. And the damage done was not as serious as anthropologists would have us believe, for cultures are constantly changing—very few are static. There is a danger today that we will go too far in accommodating the anthropologist. There are times when it seems the church growth movement is working so hard to conform to anthropological demands that the commandments of Christ and the teaching of the apostles are compromised.

Just as there are things that are harmless and perhaps even beautiful in a culture so there are things that are contrary to the gospel of Christ and the righteousness of the kingdom of God. Racism and the caste system are not sins confined to the United States alone, but are found in other cultures as well. There are practices of social and economic injustice that must be confronted both in the United States and in the Third World.

Governmental favoritism toward or the lack of proper

controls over multinational corporations are often the result of bribes. Rich landowners who exploit the Third World countries' labor markets are often protected by governments that are kept in power through the influence, and sometimes interference, of the super powers. Third World countries are caught in a vice between the competing power blocks of the East and West.

I would not mind paying high prices for coffee, gasoline, sugar, and meat if the laboring people who produce these things for us were getting a fair and just share of the profits. Missionaries need to understand economics and social and political science so that they can interpret the Scriptures that speak to these issues. Since they lack this understanding, they often take a position opposite to that which is biblically Christian.

There is a tendency for evangelicals to support the status quo, which ultimately protects the unjust cause of the rich. Similarly, the liberal often naively supports the unjust cause of the so-called Marxist or communist interests. Of course Russia, which claims to be a communist nation, displays a culture closer to that of the old Czars who exploited the laboring classes to maintain a wealthy elite. Their present leader, who is reported to have ninety-nine of the world's most expensive and luxurious automobiles, has gone even beyond the Czars. Those who think that by supporting a Russian-inspired revolution they are promoting freedom and justice for the poor and oppressed are to be pitied for their lack of knowledge.

The same can be said for those who think that by supporting the status quo they are fighting for capitalism. Karl Marx said capitalism would eventually create the means for its own destruction. He was wrong when he predicted that it would be done by an uprising of the laboring classes. The most conservative element we have in America today is the working class, which is a part of the affluent society. However, capitalism as an economic principle is in danger of being destroyed by its own successful achievements. It was built upon the principle of individual ownership of the means of production. Competition for labor would keep wages high and competition in a free market would keep prices at a minimum.

Now the means of production in many industries are no longer owned by individuals, but by stockholders of large corporations and multicorporations. These corporations are run by a managerial class that does not own the companies it serves.

In the Russian economic system the means of production are owned by the people through their government and are run by a managerial class. They have a graduated scale of wages and incentive awards for those who meet their quotas.

In the United States there is still more freedom than in Russia, even though the government now subsidizes and exercises some controls over industry. The big difference is the freedom of our workers to organize labor unions that bargain for higher pay and fringe benefits. This is not allowed in Russia and other communist countries, nor is it allowed in many of the Third World countries. We should covet for them an opportunity to increase their standards of living. We should covet the same for exploited and oppressed minorities in our own country.

It is easier for those of us who have become acquainted with the problems of minorities in the United States to understand and sympathize with Third World people than it is for some who are now serving or who have served in those countries. The Third World is just now beginning to speak out and let missionaries know what is on its mind, while blacks and others in the United States have long been calling attention to the injustices they experience. Even here, however, very little attention has been given to the condition of minorities by

Christians. Often those who serve among minorities with love and compassion do not understand the social and economic causes of their condition.

Often that which is meant to aid the poor falls far short of their needs and expectations. When the government allocates large sums of money to fight poverty the resulting programs are big and impersonal and are not really geared to the underlying causes; they are handled so impersonally they often fail to produce the desired result.

The same is true of foreign aid. The problems of Third World countries are too complex to be solved by simplistic formulas. In most of these countries wealth is concentrated in the hands of a few landowners who are protected by their governments, which are being supported by them.

Also Third World government officials are bribed by the rich and by multinational corporations so that they might be able to continue exploiting laborers and raping the land. We are not going to help the poor by going without meat or luxuries. Rather, the injustices caused through bribery must be overcome in such a way that the laboring classes will be adequately rewarded for their work, and proper provision must be made for those who cannot work.

Unless missionaries have an adequate understanding of how the gospel applies to these social, economic, and political problems they will usually be against any proposal that seeks to remedy them. At best, they will consider it outside the scope of missionary concern, which they limit to the salvation of an individual from eternal punishment. They often fail to see that genuine faith produces justice and righteousness in our public as well as in our private lives.

There is an undue emphasis in America today upon church growth, the principles of which are being transported by missionaries to the Third World. We should

want and expect churches to grow. If the biblical gospel
is preached in its fullness and in the power of the Spirit,
they will grow. However, if we compromise the gospel
in order to produce numerical results, the church becomes useless.

"Homogeneity" is a word often on the lips of those
who advocate church growth principles. It means that
we must not cross cultural, racial, or ethnic barriers to
bring people into reconciliation with each other. It as-
sumes that people who have different cultural values or
are from a different social or economic status cannot
work together in the same church. If we try to bring them
together—as did Jesus and the apostle Paul—we will
hinder the growth of the church.

I contend that if we do not bring them together we do
not have a church but a social club. Paul wrote his letters
to the Romans, Galatians, and Ephesians to show that
the Gentiles and Samaritans, despised by the Jews, had
the same opportunity to be saved at the Cross as the
Hebrews. The Jews, who boasted of a special relationship with God through the Covenant and the Law, broke
both, and were reduced to the same spiritual level as the
Gentiles. God's mercy, therefore, extended to all of His
creation, and those who are brought into one body
through Christ will form a new humanity. To compromise the gospel of reconciliation in order to produce
church growth is to defeat the purpose for which the
church was created.

The churches that are growing so rapidly in the Third
World today are those whose members evidence the
power of the Holy Spirit in their lives. The church
growth movement should emphasize social and political
science along with its study of anthropology. It should
give first priority, however, to the gospel of Jesus Christ
and the teaching of the prophets and apostles as
recorded in the Scripture. This does not necessarily
mean that all cultures should be blended into one sup-

raculture. Rather we should learn to accept and appreciate the worth and dignity of every individual who is a child of God and appreciate that which is of value in his culture. We should recognize that each has a contribution to make that will enhance and enrich our fellowship.

The call for moratorium would cease to be necessary if missionaries would esteem others better than themselves. There is much that can and should be done in recruiting and training Christian nationals. We need to subsidize new churches for them to pastor and new institutions to assist them in their ministries. But everything we do should be for the purpose of seeing the nationals use the gifts of the Holy Spirit they possess and of removing ourselves from the scene as soon as possible.

If I were in my thirties today I would do my best to change the present attitude of many missionaries and their sending churches so that control of missionary-established churches would soon be in the hands of Third World leaders.

10

Concern
for Persons

The church should not only have a pro-
phetic voice but also one that speaks to the personal and
spiritual needs of those to whom it has been called to
minister. We are not only to serve as the conscience of
society, but also to minister to individuals within society. Jesus preached to multitudes, and yet He stopped by
the side of the road to heal a blind man. He left a disap-
pointed crowd to have dinner with one man who needed
to experience the salvation that He alone could give. He
ministered to women and they ministered to Him and
witnessed to others about Him.

"How is it that you being a Jew would ask a drink of
me, a woman of Samaria?" asked the woman who had
come to draw water from the well where Jesus was rest-
ing. The reason for her question is supplied by John who
said "the Jews have no dealings with the Samaritans."
Jews looked upon Samaritans as half-breeds who wor-
shiped the God of the Hebrews while serving idols. "Are
we not right in saying," Jesus was asked on one occa-

sion, "that you are a Samaritan and have a demon?"
(John 8:48). The two were synonymous as far as Jews
were concerned.

There was another reason Jesus could have been
criticized for talking with her. She had been married and
divorced fives times and was then living with a man to
whom she was not even married.

They first discussed the difference between the Jews'
and the Samaritans' worship of God. Then Jesus dis-
creetly revealed His knowledge of her sin and she began
to recognize that He was more than an ordinary man. It
began to dawn upon her that she could be talking with
the Messiah. When she revealed her thoughts, He confessed that she was right. She immediately left her wa-
terpots and went into the village and told all the men,
"Come see a man who told me all that I have ever done. Is
this not the Messiah?" They came and believed because
of what they heard. There was a city-wide awakening
because of Jesus' interest in the salvation of a woman
who was despised and rejected by others of His race.

I once had to travel from Chicago to New York by train
for a speaking engagement because the airport in
Chicago was closed due to bad weather. At one point
during the trip, a group of men in the back of the club car
were having an animated conversation. They seemed to
be enjoying themselves so much I decided to join them.
When I did, they immediately welcomed me into their
circle and introduced themselves. All but two were medical doctors on their way home from a convention in
Chicago. One was a well-known movie star and the
other his agent. The conversation centered around Hol-
lywood and the movie industry.

After a while, most of the others retired and I was
having a personal conversation with the actor. At one
point I asked him if he belonged to a church. He replied
that he did and that he was an usher. Since it was a
church that is not well known I asked him what they

believed and how it differed from the larger denominations. When he explained their ideas, I could agree with each one of them and told him so. "But," I said, "I would need a supernatural power to live a life like that."

With a twinkle in his eye he said, "I know what you are leading up to. You are going to say I need to accept Jesus as my Lord and Savior."

He, of course, was right!

"But you would say I couldn't be a Christian," he said.

When I asked why, he said, "I have been married and divorced five times."

I asked if he had ever read the story of Jesus talking with the woman of Samaria. "She, like you," I said, "was married and divorced five times and Jesus forgave all of her sins and offered her eternal life. He called it living water: that which would satisfy the thirst of her soul."

As I explained how the woman had been searching all her life for satisfaction which she had been unable to find and how Jesus was able to provide that which would meet her need, this man, who makes millions laugh as a comedian, began to cry. As tears rolled down his cheeks his manager suggested they go to their room. He demurred saying, "Our conversation is too important."

We remained until after midnight talking about the love and compassion Jesus has for all people including men like himself. He was very close to the kingdom of God when we finally parted.

He has told about accepting Jesus Christ as his Lord and Savior on television talk shows since our conversation, but I have not seem him or heard from him. I do not know if he has had a genuine conversion experience or not. I do know that all who repent and confess their sins and embrace Jesus Christ as Lord will receive God's forgiveness because of Christ's atoning sacrifice on the cross.

Jesus met the spiritual needs of many others who were despised by men. One sinful woman came and anointed the feet of Jesus as He sat in the house of a Pharisee. Jesus informed her that her sins were forgiven.

Zacchaeus was a publican and a sinner. A publican was a tax collector for the Roman government, which had invaded Israel and made it a part of its empire. Zacchaeus was a traitor and a crook, one of the most despised persons in the nation. People murmured when Jesus stopped a procession and went home to eat with him. During the visit, Zacchaeus was transformed by the power of God. To prove that his profession was real, he promised to return everything he had taken by fraud and to give half of his wealth to the poor (Luke 19:1–10).

We need to be ready to share these accounts of Jesus' mercy and compassion with those we meet along the way.

There is only one way to clear a guilty conscience and that is to come to Jesus by faith. "If we confess our sins, he is faithful and just, and will forgive our sins and cleanse us from all unrighteousness" (1 John 1:9).

Jesus Heals the Sick and Gives Proof to the Doubtful

A nurse in Detroit often attended the morning worship service of the church I served as pastor. She and her mother belonged to an extremely liberal church, but it was such a long distance from their home they often attended ours, which was within walking distance.

Upon my first visit to her home, the nurse told me she was working for her degree in philosophy at Wayne State University. She also told me she enjoyed my preaching but did not agree with my belief in the miracles of the Bible. We had an interesting discussion concerning this and other topics.

Within a few days after my visit I learned she was in

the hospital. I immediately went to see her. She was very sick. It was evident she did not feel well enough for a prolonged visit. I quoted two verses of Scripture, offered a brief prayer, and said I would return when she was feeling better.

A few days later I discovered she was home and I went to see her. She met me at the door and said, "Pastor, when you were here before I told you I did not believe in miracles. When you gave illustrations of God answering prayer I always thought it was just a coincidence, but now I know better. I was suffering from a high fever when you visited me in the hospital. I had undergone surgery and was to have another operation. When you prayed, the fever left, and I immediately felt better. The doctor came an hour later and after an examination said, 'I do not know what has happened but you do not need to have the second operation.' "

She said, "As a nurse I knew what was wrong with me and I know I am home today not because of a coincidence but because of God's miracle-working power. I thought of Thomas who when told that Jesus had risen from the dead said, 'Unless, I see in his hands the print of the nails, and place my finger in the mark of the nails, and place my hand in his side, I will not believe' " (John 20:24, 25).

Not everyone I have prayed for in my lifetime has been healed in such a miraculous manner as the nurse. But some have been, and I can testify to a similar miracle in my own life.

There are many good people who, like Thomas and the nurse, must have rational proof before they will believe. Of course, it is not possible to prove by rational argument that God exists or that Jesus is the Son of God and the Savior of the world. But it is possible to show that a rational person can come to this conclusion and that ours is not a blind but a reasonable faith.

Throughout my ministry I have tried to listen sympathetically as people informed me of their doubts and the reasons for them. I have not tried to brush them off with a glib or sarcastic remark. We need to learn to listen to honest questions and be ready with honest answers.

If I were in my thirties today I would want to keep informed on subjects that are of interest to young adults studying for graduate and post-graduate degrees. When I go to a university, I like to browse in the bookstores and find out which books are most popular among students. By reading these I am able to learn what is of interest to the students at that particular time. The beliefs of students and their attitudes toward life are changing from year to year. Jesus' ministry to the woman of Samaria was effective because He knew all about her. He knew all persons and what they were thinking. If we are to be effective disciples, we need to know as much as possible about the people we have been called to serve.

We do not have the knowledge of Jesus, but we can learn a great deal about people through reading and personal contact. We should gain knowledge not to increase our prestige among intellectuals but to be in a better position to meet the spiritual needs of others.

Most people are not intellectuals, and the barriers that have been erected between them and God are not intellectual but emotional. Many times they have had a bad experience with religious people in the past and they are rejecting God or the church because of this experience.

I once enjoyed a stimulating conversation with an executive of a magazine that was very popular a few years ago. We were sitting across from each other in the dining car of a train. I listened as he told me about the places he had been and the things he had seen. I had visited most of them myself in the course of my ministry and enjoyed discussing them with him.

Suddenly he asked me what kind of work I did. When I told him I was a minister of the gospel he immediately replied, "I have no use for God or the church."

That did not shock me; I had heard it before. I said, "I am interested in people and their attitudes toward religion. Please forget that I am a minister and tell me very frankly why you do not believe in God. Whatever you say will not hurt my feelings or cause me to think any less of you as a person."

He said that he belonged to a church and attended services regularly until he was drafted for military service. Even then he attended chapel services regularly. The chaplain was a minister from his own denomination. He said, "I was sincere in my religious beliefs, but it soon became evident he was not.

"When I was released from the service I was to get married. The day before the wedding I talked with my fiance's pastor and told him the marriage would not work. He advised me to go ahead with the ceremony, as it was too late to back out now. 'You can get a divorce later,' he said."

I cannot imagine why a pastor would give that kind of advice, but this one did and the ceremony took place. This man's wife later became a psychopathic case and they were divorced.

He said, "You see, religion failed me each time I was facing a crisis in my life. This is why I do not believe in God or attend church."

I told him I did not blame him for feeling the way he did about the church and religion. "But," I said, "have you ever read the Bible to see what Jesus Christ was like and what the church should be like."

He said, "No, I never have."

Then I began to tell him about the love and compassion of Jesus Christ and of the deep understanding He had of people and His concern for the salvation of an individual.

He listened and finally said, "In all my life, I have never heard this from anyone. No one ever told me before." "This," he remarked, "is the real thing, it is practical. The ministers I have known have always been up in the air, but what you have presented is down to earth where I live."

There are many people who are very successful in their businesses or professional lives, but who are very lonely and hollow inside. They need to talk to someone who will listen sympathetically and who will then tell them about Jesus and who will show them how He can meet their individual needs. "Come to me, all who labor and are heavy laden," Jesus pleaded, "and I will give you rest. Take my yoke upon you, and learn from me; for I am gentle and lowly in heart, and you will find rest for your souls. For my yoke is easy, and my burden is light" (Matt. 11:28–30).

Cities are filled with lonely people. Some are poor, others are rich, but all need to know the Savior.

There are those who are mentally and physically handicapped. Jesus had a special concern for them when he was on earth and He still wants to minister to them through us. The public facilities that are provided for those who cannot be cared for at home are large and impersonal. These, of all people, need individual attention and loving concern. There should be places of employment for those who are able to work so they can provide their own support and maintain a healthy self-image. There are those who are retired on a small social security allotment with no pension to supplement it. They also need individual attention, love, and friendship.

There are so many different kinds of people with needs, such as widows, divorcees, and orphans. Jesus loves them and wants to give them individual attention through His church. "As the Father has sent me, even so I send you" (John 20:21). This He told His disciples prior to His departure to be with His Father.

If I were in my thirties, I would try to get the church to reexamine its priorities in the light of the needs of these lonely people.

11

Plan for the Future

America may be heading toward what Robert Bellah describes as "her third great time of trial." If he is right, and I personally believe he is, the third great awakening began in the sixties and will continue to grow in depth and intensity. It will bring about a reawakening of the conscience of our citizens and will change the churches that are open to renewal and replace those that are not.

New churches are already being formed. They are small and may seem inconsequential now, but they are growing, whereas many of the traditional churches are losing support. Old programs that have been highly successful in the past will give way to new and more innovative methods of evangelism and training. The Sunday school and Sunday evening service, though still meeting peoples' needs in some churches, are holding on only as a tradition in others.

When a business has a popular product that is making a profit, a good executive will be planning ahead for he knows that its popularity will not last. He must have a new product to take its place before the sales begin to decline. The church should take the same attitude toward any of its methods that seem to be working now. These will eventually lose their appeal and effectiveness. Therefore, we should be keeping up with the trends of society and trying to discern which of these are temporary and which of them will be more permanent. The latter should be projected into the future. New programs should be devised that will be more relevant to the projected life-styles and desires of people in the future. It is not as easy to do this today as it was a few years ago. Things are rapidly changing and life becomes more unpredictable all the time.

Because of the uncertainty of this present era, business executives who used to project their plans on a five-year basis are now cutting down to two. Although we should endeavor to plan ahead further than two years at a time, we should also be flexible and ready to change our plans as soon as we discover the inaccuracy of our predictions or the inadequacy of our programs.

If the present spiritual renewal continues and produces widespread repentance and the desire to correct social, economic, and judical injustices and a strong, dedicated minority committed to implementing needed changes, then we need to prepare for some revolutionary adjustments in the entire structure of society. We as Christians should do everything we can to see that the changes are made peacefully. Tensions among the so-called underclass have been building up for a period of time and it looks as though we are now about to reach the breaking point. A recent *Time* magazine article reported that nearly one-half of the black population in the United States has now attained middle-class status. But this has only increased the anger and frustration of the other half whose economic situation is getting worse instead of better.[1]

[1]"Looking for a Reason," *Time*, July 25, 1977, p. 17.

Recently there was a riot in Chicago's Humboldt Park. It was a repetition of the riots in the same area during the sixties. Cars were overturned, windows were smashed, stores were burned, people were killed, many were injured, and over one hundred were arrested. This was also accompanied by looting and all the other ugly things that characterize a riot of this proportion in a large city on a warm summer evening. But there was one marked difference between this one and that of the sixties. The former was started by blacks. This was started by Puerto Ricans. There are other ethnic groups suffering from discrimination and lack of employment. Tensions that provide a potential for even greater catastrophies are mounting.

When we add to these tensions the lack of public confidence in the leaders of government and the economic squeeze being felt by the middle class as a result of inflation, we have all the ingredients of a major uprising in this country that could be comparable in scope to the Civil War. In the light of this possibility, what should we as a church be doing? What is our responsibility and how do we carry it out?

Be Prophetic

The church must give up its courtship with the world if it is to fulfill the task committed to it by God. We have arrived at the place in history where we need the voice of a prophet. This is not a popular role for the preacher. You cannot win friends and influence people by calling attention to their sins and the impending judgment that is certain unless they repent. People do not want to be told that America is under the condemnation of God any more than the people of Israel wanted to hear the pronouncements of Jeremiah concerning their impending captivity by an idolatrous nation.

We are like Habakkuk who prayed, "O Lord, how long shall I cry for help, and thou wilt not hear? Or cry to thee 'Violence!' and thou wilt not save? Why dost thou make me see wrongs and look upon trouble? Destruction and violence are before me; strife and contention arise. So the law is slacked and justice never goes forth; for the wicked surround the righteous, so justice goes forth perverted" (Hab. 1:1–4).

When God answered the prophet by saying, "I am rousing the Chalde'ans, that bitter and hasty nation, who march through the earth, to seize habitations not their own," (Hab. 1:6) and said He was going to use them to punish Israel, Habakkuk didn't like it. "O, Lord my God, my Holy One, why have you ordained them for judgment? Why are you chastising Israel with them? You are of purer eyes than to behold evil and cannot look upon wrong. Why do you look upon men without faith, and remain silent when the wicked swallow up the person more righteous than he?" (Hab. 1:12, 13, paraphrase).

We recognize and complain about that which is wrong with our nation, but we still like to think that it is more righteous than others. We do not like to be told that we are in danger of becoming the captive of an enemy nation far worse than our own. Therefore, the person who sounds the alarm will pay the consequences. Yet if the minister of the gospel is to be true to his calling, he must include a prophetic note in his preaching.

We should become sensitive to the cries of the poor and the oppressed minorities in our midst. We can no longer afford to enjoy the luxuries of our affluent society and ignore their plight as though it did not exist or was not our responsibility. We like to salve our conscience by walling ourselves off from their sight and pretending that poverty and suffering is their own fault.

Professing Christians have told me that if the poor were as industrious as they are, they could then enjoy prosperity comparable to their own. This reveals callous indifference toward the poor and willful ignorance of the causes of poverty. God will not tolerate such arrogance for long. Belonging to an evangelical church and professing to have Jesus as Savior will not save people like this from the judgment of God. We must do what we can to make them aware of their false sense of security and call them to repentance and confession of sins before it is too late. This we must do for two reasons: we love them, and we love our nation. We want to save both from disaster that is sure to come unless there is true repentance and submission to Jesus Christ as Lord.

We can become aware of what the problems are by reading books and articles pertaining to poverty and discrimination. We can establish personal friendships with blacks and other minorities, listen to their complaints, and then look for biblical solutions. We should then do what we can to communicate our knowledge and call attention to the Scriptures that pertain to social, economic, judicial, and political righteousness. We can encourage each other to make decisions and take actions in our business, professional, or community relationships that will be in accord with the justice of God's kingdom.

Reconciliation

The disciples of Jesus Christ are called to be ambassadors of God and ministers of reconciliation. When Jesus died on the cross, God was in Christ reconciling the world unto Himself (2 Cor. 5:19). As men are reconciled to God, they are also reconciled to each other. The church then serves as a model of brotherhood so that all the world can witness what it will be like in the coming kingdom and how they can live in peace and harmony with each other now. We have a ministry to our nation and the world. It is our task to do our best to understand, through reading and personal contact, the various cultures within the United States and the other nations of the world.

When people riot, the natural tendency is to demand more police or military protection. This is sometimes necessary. However, we who are Christians should recognize it as a temporary solution that is only appealed to as a last resort. We should try to avoid permitting a situation ever coming to this kind of a confrontation.

The failure of social engineers to solve problems in the past should not deter us from continuing our efforts to create an economy that will provide for the basic necessities of all our fellow citizens. But we should seek to do this in a way that will preserve dignity and self-respect. There has been a plan for reforming the welfare system in Washington for several years. I hope the political obstacles that keep it from being passed will soon be overcome. When it does come before Congress, Christians ought to show their commitment to the teaching of Jesus Christ by encouraging their congressional representatives to vote favorably. If there are flaws, and there no doubt will be, provision should be made for their removal.

It should be possible to work out an economic system where all those who are able to work at some gainful employment will have an opportunity to do so. Since many women are now working outside the home, often taking jobs that only men have held in the past, our aim should be to make more jobs available. It is unfortunate that many families with two incomes enjoy extra cars and other luxuries while other men and women are unable to find employment.

There are, of course, many women who are the heads of households and are working to provide food, clothing, and shelter for themselves and their children. This requires more money than women are usually paid. A strictly enforced and adequate minimum wage would keep women from being hired only because their labor is cheaper and at the same time would provide for the basic needs of those who qualify for a particular job.

It may be necessary to shorten the work week. This might decrease the family income but would provide more time for both husband and wife to be with their children. I am not an economist, but I know that as long as we continue to live in a society that believes in the work ethic, there needs to be an opportunity for people to be gainfully employed for the sake of their own personal esteem and for the good of society.

Employment is only one of the concerns of the minorities. Many of them are endeavoring to preserve their ethnic and cultural identities while adjusting to a new culture and environment. Many times their children are attending our schools without first having a basic course in English. People of minority communities say very little about the schools or the problems that arise there; they feel their lives are controlled by outside and impersonal forces. The poor see all the luxuries enjoyed by middle-class suburbanites and contrast this with their own drab existence. Middle-class Christians should do what they can to bridge the gap between the people in these communities and those in our own.

More important perhaps than anything we can do in the way of programs is the *attitude* we can help create among our associates and those we influence. If we are fully informed about and in personal contact with people of other racial or ethnic groups, we can appreciate the things of value within their culture. Many of us Anglo-Saxons have come to enjoy Italian, Spanish, and Oriental food. A little exploration would reveal other things from other cultures that would bring variety and enrichment to our lives.

"Why did God make us so different?" said a young woman sitting next to me on a plane. Her father was an American black and her mother was German. She had applied for an apartment on the North Shore Drive in Chicago. The manager said they could accept her because her skin was white but she would not be able to entertain her friends who are black. This was only one of many problems she encountered. I replied that we need variety among people as well as among flowers. How much more beautiful is the flower garden that has a mixture of different kinds and colors of flowers.

We are robbing ourselves of the beauty of God's creation when we fail to see the contribution that is made to society by the different colors and kinds of people God has placed in the world. Our task as Christians is to call attention to that beauty.

Home

The breakdown of authority has produced an unhappy situation in the homes of America. Women have more liberty today because of the pill, opportunity for equal education with men, and the beginning of an increased status and opportunity in the business and professional world.

Children have less restraint and not as much care and attention from parents. There is very little for them to do to occupy their time constructively. When parents are divorced, which is an increasing problem, a child's self-esteem is damaged and all kinds of problems may emerge as a result. And parents who nave ceased to love and respect each other but continue to live together cannot help but manifest their feelings to the children and this also has a detrimental effect upon their lives.

There will be even greater emotional and mental problems in the future as a result of the lack of a permanent commitment between couples who are living together without the traditional marriage ceremony and legal involvements.

The church should be prepared to give the counseling

and care that is needed to repair the damage of broken homes, broken hearts, and broken lives.

Television

Television has been both a blessing and a curse. It has brought the world closer together and enabled us to learn more about other peoples and places. It has also provided the opportunity for us to keep up with politics and current events. At the same time it has produced excitement that has made school and church rather dull and boring unless the teachers and ministers have personalities similar to actors and actresses. It has decreased the desire to read good literature and has hindered communication in the home and among friends.

Television networks will continue to provide us with a steady diet of sex and violence unless Christians can offer creative alternative programming. There is an urgent need for Christian television script writers and producers who can create prime-time programming that adheres to biblical principles of morality. The church needs to make this need known, especially to its young people.

Christians should also take time to write to networks, producers, sponsors, and local stations commending them for good programs and expressing specific criticisms of poor or distasteful programs. The church should encourage and perhaps even instruct its members to take a responsible interest in this medium which has become such a powerful influence in the lives of both children and adults.

Pastoral Leadership

There is a lack of good leadership within the church and this is of serious concern to me as I try to project my thinking and plans into the future. Seminaries are preparing young persons for teaching but not for preaching and administering a church. The curriculum was designed for the fifties not for the seventies and eighties. Young men who recognize that many of the present churches are not meeting the spiritual needs of people are relying too much upon fads based upon the latest theories of pop psychology. Pastors often do not depend upon the Holy Spirit and the power of God's Word to reach the consciences of their congregations who in that same Spirit can make the necessary corrections in the institutions of society.

Many people have lost their respect for pastoral leadership. Lay persons are meeting in homes and joining informal groups because their spiritual needs are not being met in church. In many cases this is due to the shortcomings of pastors who do not have a thorough knowledge of God's Word and its applicability to contemporary issues.

If I were in my thirties, I would give a more central place to the church of Jesus Christ and less importance to independent organizations that criticise the church structures from which they receive their support.

I would seek to restructure our seminaries so they would be more responsible to the churches and more responsive to their needs. Their students would be more carefully selected to include only those who had gifts of preaching, teaching, church administration, and a genuine love for people. They would be trained to use their gifts to help people relate to God and others and to serve as models of the future kingdom that is to be established over all the earth.

My fear is that some of the more successful movements have come under the influence and control of wealthy individuals and foundations and right-wing politicians. As a result, they preach the false gospel of easy believism while opposing the righteousness and justice of the kingdom of God taught by the Lord Jesus, the apostles, and the prophets.

Genetics

New discoveries of science in the realm of genetics should cause us to give some serious thought to the moral and spiritual problems involved. If, as now seems possible, scientists are able to establish or change the sex and even the personality of a child prior to birth, is this going to be for the benefit of society? Who will make the decisions? If B. F. Skinner's predictions for our technocratic society in his book *Beyond Freedom and Dignity* should be fulfilled, who within humankind is capable of playing God? Shall it be politicians elected by the people? Who should they choose as their technical advisors? Or shall we have a society run by professional psychiatrists? Could Skinner be trusted to make the important decisions? If I were in my thirties, I would want to be prepared with objective answers to some of these questions by the time the decisions have to be made.

In the past, the church has first reacted against new scientific and technological discoveries; then it becomes silent, and finally the church accepts what it first opposed. (Television is a good example. Many evangelicals were opposed to it and now we are as addicted as anyone else.)

War and Peace

The Bible does not give us a simple moral principle regarding Christian involvement in war. What attitude should the Christian have toward war? Is war ever justified? If so, under what conditions? If not, how should national and international security be assured?

In Luke 22:36 Jesus told his disciples that if they had no swords, they should sell their garments and buy them. In Matthew 10:34 He told them He had come not to bring peace but a sword. Yet when Peter cut off the ear of the high priest's servant, Jesus rebuked him saying, "Put your sword back into place; for all who take the sword will perish by the sword" (Matt. 26:52).

These questions and seeming contradictions need to be studied objectively and prayerfully in an age when a nuclear holocaust is a very real possibility.

The Bible

Current discussions concerning the inspiration and authority of Scripture should be of paramount importance to young evangelicals. They should be aware of the mistakes that liberals have made in the past and the reasons that fundamentalists and evangelicals take a high view of the inspiration of Scripture.

The issues raised by both sides should be taken seriously and objectively and without rancor or personal vindictiveness. A wrong way of stating or defending a truth can be tragic. Because of fear of rejection, people are reluctant to press ideas contrary to those of the group to which they belong. Consequently, many times they remain silent until the people they look to for leadership change their positions.

Let's not be afraid to face the hard questions. We must face them in love and in a spirit of humility, with a desire not to prove a point but to discover what the Bible claims and how we should respond to these claims.

These are only a few of the issues I see that will affect the future. Young evangelicals should develop answers carefully and diligently. They should also possess the ability and courage to communicate these answers in a way that will make a difference in the church and in society.

If I were in my thirties today I would seek to avoid the mistakes of the past, overcome the apathy and cynicism of the present, and provide a hope for the future through the preaching of the Good News concerning the kingdom.

I would pray in the words of the Psalmist, "Wilt thou not revive us again, that thy people may rejoice in thee?" (Ps. 85:6).

I believe with the writer of this Psalm that "God the Lord . . . will speak peace to his people, to his saints, to those who turn to him in their hearts" (Ps. 85:8). When spiritual renewal comes to our churches it will be reflected in the music of the choir and the singing of the congregation. Instead of expressing our worship through words and tunes written two or three centuries ago, we will be expressing the deep feelings implanted in our hearts by the Holy Spirit through contemporary language and music. The preaching, instead of being a series of pious platitudes or harangues against styles of clothing or length of hair, will be delivered in the power and demonstration of the Holy Spirit. Pastors will reveal what God's Word has to say against the sins of adultery, drunkenness, selfishness, greed, oppression, injustice, and inequality.

There will be tears of grief and sorrow as people repent of their sins. There will be tears and shouts of joy as people receive God's forgiveness and cleansing.

When renewal comes it will have an effect upon the personal and corporate morality of the nation and the world, and it will provide a spiritual foundation for the new culture that is now in the process of being formed. You who are now in your thirties will be the leaders in this movement of the Spirit—a movement that will affect all ages and classes of people. It is to you that I offer my prayers of support.

Selected Bibliography

CHAPTER 1

Beach, Waldo. *Conscience on Campus.* New York: Associated Press, 1966.

Cantelon, John E. *A Protestant Approach to the Campus Ministry.* Philadelphia: Westminster Press, n.d.

Cohen, Daniel. *The New Believers.* New York: Ballantine Books, 1975.

Cohen, Mitchell, and Hale, Dennis, eds. *The New Student Left.* Revised ed. Boston: Beacon, 1967.

Cowles Education Corporation. *Youth Quake.* New York: Cowles Education Corporation, 1967.

Cullman, Oscar. *Jesus and the Revolutionaries.* New York: Harper and Row Publishers, Inc., 1970.

Dyal, William M., Jr. *It's Worth Your Life.* New York: Association Press, 1967.

Friedenberg, Edgar Z. *The Vanishing Adolescent.* New York: Dell Publishing Co., Inc., 1962.

Goodman, Paul. *Growing Up Absurd.* New York: Random Press, 1960.

Josselyn, Irene M. *The Adolescent and His World.* New York: Family Service Association of America, 1964.

Kelman, Steven. *Push Comes to Shove.* Boston: Houghton Mifflin Co., 1970.

Kennan, George F. *Democracy and the Student Left.* New York: Bantam Books, 1968.

Kenniston, Kenneth. *Young Radicals.* New York: Harcourt, Brace and Ward, Inc., 1968.

Knight, Walter, compiler. *Jesus People Come Alive.* Wheaton, Illinois: Tyndale House Publishers, 1971.

McClellan, Grant S. *American Youth in a Changing Culture.* New York: H. W. Wilson Co., 1972.

McCoy, Charles S. *The Gospel On Campus.* Atlanta: John Knox Press, 1959.

Moore, Peter C. *Youth in Crisis.* New York: Seabury Press, 1966.

Proctor, William. *Survival On Campus: A Handbook for Christian Students.* Old Tappan, New Jersey: Fleming H. Revell Co., 1972.

Reich, Charles A. *The Greening of America.* New York: Bantam Publishers, 1971.

Rogan, Donald L. *Campus Apocalypse.* New York: Seabury Press, 1969.

Roszak, Theordore. *The Making of A Counter Culture.* New York: Doubleday and Co., Inc., Anchor Books, 1969.

Salisbury, Harrison E. *The Shook Up Generation.* Chicago: Fawcett Publications, 1963.

Slauson, S. R. *Re-Educating the Delinquent.* Don Mills, Ontario: Collier-MacMillan Canada, Ltd., Collier Books, 1961.

Tunley, Roul. *Kids Crime and Chaos: A World Report on Juvenile Delinquency.* New York: Dell Publishing Co., 1964.

Voellkel, Harold. *Student Evangelism in a World of Revolution.* Grand Rapids, Michigan: Zondervan Publishing House, 1974.

Wallis, Jim. *Agenda for Biblical People.* New York: Harper and Row, 1976.

CHAPTER 2

Beardsley, Frank Greenville. *Religious Progress Through Religious Revivals.* New York: American Tract Society, 1943.

Bellah, Robert N. *The Broken Covenant: American Civil Religion in Time of Trial.* New York: Seabury Press, Crossroad Books, 1975.

Bouldriej, Kenneth E. *The Meaning of the Twentieth Century.* New York: Harper and Row Publishers, Inc., 1965.

Brinton, Crane. *The Shaping of Modern Thought.* Englewood Cliffs, New Jersey: Prentice-Hall, 1963.

Burns, James. *Revivals, Their Laws and Their Leaders.* Grand Rapids, Michigan: Baker Book House, 1960.

Carse, James. *Jonathan Edwards and The Visibility of God.* New York: Charles Scribner's Sons, 1967.

Cell, Edward. *Religion and Contemporary Western Culture.* Nashville: Abingdon Press, 1967.

Ellul, Jacques. *Hope in Time of Abandonment.* New York: Seabury Press, 1973.

Finney, Charles G. *Autobiography.* Old Tappan, New Jersey: Fleming H. Revell Co., 1975.

Finney, Charles G. *Love Is Not a Special Way of Feeling.* Minneapolis: Bethany Fellowship, Dimension Books, 1963.

Finney, Charles G. *Revival Fire.* Waukesha, Wisconsin: Metropolitan Church Association: Reprint ed., Minneapolis: Bethany Fellowship, n.d.

Heilbroner, Robert L. *The Future as History.* New York: Harper and Row, 1968.

Henry, Carl F. H. *The Remaking of the Modern Mind.* Grand Rapids, Michigan: Wm. B. Eerdmans, 1946.

Hirvey, G. E., *Manual of Revivals.* New York: Funk and Wagnalls, 1884.

Hudson, Winthrop. *The Great Tradition of the American Churches.* New York: Harper and Row Publishers, Inc., Harper Torch Books, 1953.

James, William. *Varieties of Religious Experience.* London: Longmans Green and Company, 1902.

Latourettes, Kenneth Scott. *Christianity Through the Ages.* New York: Harper and Row Publishers, Inc., Harper Chappel Books, 1965.

Lukacs, John. *The Passing of the Modern Age.* New York: Harper and Row Publishers, Inc., 1970.

Marty, Martin. *Righteous Empire: The Protestant Experience in America.* New York: The Dial Press, Inc., 1970.

Marty, Martin. *The Pro and Con Book of Religious America: A Bicentennial Argument*. Waco, Texas. Word Books, 1975.

Marty, Martin. *The Fire We Can Light*. New York: Doubleday, 1973.

May, Rollo. *Power and Innocence: A Search for the Sources of Violence*. New York: W. W. Norton and Co., Inc., 1972.

Montgomery, John Warwick. *The Shaping of the Past*. Minneapolis: Bethany Fellowship, 1975.

Murphy, Ian H. *The Puritan Hope*. Carlisle, Pennsylvania: The Banner of Truth Trust, 1971.

Olmstead, Clifton E. *Religion in America: Past and Present*. Englewood Cliffs, New Jersey: Prentice-Hall, Inc., Spectrum, 1961.

Outler, Albert. *Evangelism in the Wesleyan Spirit*. Nashville, Tennessee: Tidings, 1971.

Phares, Ross. *Bible in Pocket, Gun in Hand: The Story of Frontier Religion*. Lincoln, Nebraska: University of Nebraska Press, 1971.

Schrag, Peter. *The Decline of the WASP*. New York: Simon and Schuster, 1973.

Smith, John E. *Religious Affections: Works of Jonathan Edwards*, Volume 2. New Haven: Yale University Press, 1959.

Sweet, William Warren. *Revivalism in America*. Magnolia, Maryland: Peter Smith, Publisher Inc., 1944.

Trueblood, Elton. *The Predicament of Modern Man*. New York: Harper and Row Publishers, Inc., 1944.

Von Barth, Herbert. *The Unfinished Society*. New York: Hawthorne Books, 1962.

Walsh, Chad. *From Utopia to Nightmare*. London: Geoffrey Bles, 1962.

Wheelis, Allen. *The End of the Modern Age*. New York: Harper and Row Publishers, Inc., 1972.

"America's Great Revivals." Minneapolis: Bethany Fellowship, Inc. Reprinted from *Christian Life Magazine*, n.d.

CHAPTER 3

Bloesch, Donald G. *The Crises of Piety*. Grand Rapids, Michigan: Wm. B. Eerdmans, 1968.

Bloesch, Donald G. *The Evangelical Renaissance*. Grand Rapids, Michigan: Wm. B. Eerdmans, 1973.

Bloesch, Donald G. *The Invaded Church*. Waco, Texas: Word Books, 1975.

Carnell, Edward John. *The Case for Orthodox Theology*. Philadelphia: Westminster Press, 1959.

Cauthen, Kenneth. *The Impact of American Religious Liberalism*. New York: Harper and Row Publishers, Inc., 1962.

Cobb, John B. *Liberal Christianity at the Crossroads*. Philadelphia: Westminster Press, 1973.

Dollar, George W. *A History of Fundamentalism in America*. Greenville, South Carolina: Bob Jones University Press, 1973.

Fosdick, Harry Emerson. *The Living of These Days: An Autobiography*. New York: Harper and Row Publishers, Inc., 1956.

Glad, Paul W., ed. *William Jennings Bryan*. New York: Farrar, Straus, and Giroux, Inc., Hill and Wang, 1968.

Henry, Carl F. H. *Basic Christian Doctrines*. Toronto: Holt, Rinehart and Winston of Canada, Ltd., 1962; reprint ed., Grand Rapids, Michigan: Baker Book House, 1971.

Henry, Carl F. H. *The Uneasy Conscience of Modern Fundamentalism*. Grand Rapids, Michigan: Wm. B. Eerdmans, 1947.

Hordern, William E. *A Layman's Guide to Protestant Theology*. Toronto: MacMillan Company of Canada, Ltd., 1968.

Jorstad, Erling. *The Politics of Doomsday: The Fundamentalists of the Far Right*. Nashville: Abingdon Press, 1970.

Lloyd-Jones, D. Martin. *Truth Unchanged, Unchanging*. Old Tappan, New Jersey: Fleming H. Revell Co., 1947.

Machen, Greshan J. *Christianity and Liberalism*. Grand Rapids, Michigan: Wm. B. Eerdmans, 1946.

Mackintosh, Hugh Ross. *Types of Modern Theology*. New York: Charles Scribner's Sons, 1937.

Moberg, David O. *The Great Reversal*. Philadelphia: J. P. Lippincott Co., A. J. Holman Co., 1972.

Murch, James DeForest. *Protestant Revolt*. Arlington, Virginia: Crestwood Books, n.d.

Pierard, Richard R. *The Unequal Yoke*. Philadelphia: J. B. Lippincott Co., 1970.

Ramm, Bernard L. *The Evangelical Heritage*. Waco, Texas: Word Books, 1973.

Roy, Ralph Lord. *Apostles of Discord*. Boston: The Beacon Press, 1953.

Russell, Allyn C. *Voices of American Fundamentalism*. Philadelphia: Westminster Press, 1976.

Shelley, Bruce. *Evangelicalism in America*. Grand Rapids, Michigan: Wm. B. Eerdmans, 1967.

Van Dusen, Henry. *The Vindication of Liberal Theology*. New York: Charles Scribner's Sons, 1963.

Walker, Alan, *The New Evangelism*. Nashville: Abingdon Press, 1975.

Walker, Brooks R. *The Christian Fright Peddlers*. New York: Doubleday and Co., Inc., 1975.

Wells, David F., and Woodbridge, John D. *The Evangelicals: What They Believe, Who They Are, Where They Are Changing*. Nashville: Abingdon Press, 1975.

CHAPTER 4

Bright, John. *The Kingdom of God*. Nashville: Abingdon Press, 1953.

Dodd, C. H. *The Parables of the Kingdom*. New York: Charles Scribner's Sons, 1961.

Ellul, Jacques. *The False Presence of the Kingdom*. New York: Seabury Press, 1972.

Ellul, Jacques. *The Presence of the Kingdom*. New York: Seabury Press, 1967.

Ellul, Jacques. *The Political Illusion*. New York: Vintage Books of Random House, 1972.

Emerson, William A., Jr. *Sin and the New American Conscience*. New York: Harper and Row Publishers, Inc., 1974.

Evans, Louis H. *The Kingdom Is Yours*. Old Tappan, New Jersey: Fleming H. Revell Co., n.d.

Hatfield, Mark. *Conflict and Conscience*. Waco, Texas: Word Books, 1971.

Heilbroner, Robert L. *An Inquiry into the Human Prospect*. New York: W. W. Norton and Co., 1974.

Ladd, George Eldon. *Jesus Christ and History*. Downers Grove, Illinois: Inter-Varsity Press, 1963.

Niebuhr, Richard H. *The Kingdom of God in America*. New York: Harper and Row Publishers, Inc., Torch Books, 1937.

CHAPTER 5

Berger, Peter L. *The Noise of Solemn Assemblies.* New York: Doubleday and Co., Inc., 1961.

Berton, Pierre. *The Comfortable Pew.* New York: J. B. Lippincott Co., 1965.

Come, Arnold B. *Agents of Reconciliation.* Philadelphia: Westminster Press, 1964.

DeWolf, Harold L. *A Hard Rain and a Cross.* Nashville: Abingdon Press, 1960.

Fuller, Reginald H., and Rice, Brian K. *Christianity and the Affluent Society.* Grand Rapids, Michigan: Wm. B. Eerdmans, 1966.

Gilkey, Langdon. *How the Church Can Minister to the World Without Losing Itself.* New York: Harper and Row Publishers, Inc., 1964.

Gillquist, Peter E. *Love is Now.* Grand Rapids, Michigan: Zondervan Publishing House, 1970.

Grounds, Vernon. *Revolution and the Christian Faith.* New York: J. B. Lippincott Company, Holman Books, 1971.

Hadden, Jeffrey K. *The Gathering Storm.* New York: Doubleday and Co., Inc., 1969.

Haselden, Kyle, and Marty, Martin, eds. *What's Ahead for the Churches.* Chicago: The Christian Century, 1963.

Hill, Samuel S., Jr. *Southern Churches in Crisis.* Toronto: Holt, Rinehart and Winston of Canada, Ltd., 1966.

Hoekendijk, J. C. *The Church Inside Out.* Philadelphia: Westminster Press, 1966.

Hudnut, Robert K. *The Sleeping Giant: Arousing Church Power in America.* New York: Harper and Row Publishers, Inc., 1971.

Hunt, George Laird. *Rediscovering the Church.* New York: National Board of the Young Men's Christian Association, 1956. (2nd printing. New York: Association Press, 1958.)

Jacobson, Marion Leach. *Saints and Snobs.* Wheaton, Illinois: Tyndale House Publishers, 1972.

Kelbourn, William, ed. *The Restless Church.* New York: J. B. Lippincott Co., 1966.

Klemme, Huber F. *Your Church and Your Community.* Philadelphia: Christian Education Press, 1957.

Lee, Robert, and Galloway, Russell, eds. *Schizophrenic Church: Conflict Over Community Organization.* Philadelphia: Westminster Press, 1969.

McLaughlin, Raymond W. *Communication for the Churches.* Grand Rapids, Michigan: Zondervan Publishing House, 1968.

McNeil, Jesse J. *Mission in Metropolis.* Grand Rapids, Michigan: Wm. B. Eerdmans, 1965.

Menninger, Karl. *Whatever Became of Sin?* New York: Hawthorne Books, 1973.

Oden, Thomas C. *Beyond Revolution.* Philadelphia: Westminster Press, n.d.

Richards, Lawrence. *A New Face for the Church.* Grand Rapids, Michigan: Zondervan Publishing House, 1970.

Shedd, Russell Phillip. *Man in Community.* Grand Rapids, Michigan: Wm. B. Eerdmans, 1964.

Shippey, Frederick A. *Protestantism and Suburban Life.* Nashville: Abingdon Press, 1964.

Snyder, Howard A. *The Problem of Wineskins: Church Renewal in a Technological Age.* Downers Grove, Illinois: Inter-Varsity Press, 1975. (2nd printing)

Webber, George W. *God's Colony in Man's World.* Nashville: Abingdon Press, 1960.

Webber, George W. *The Congregation in Mission.* Nashville: Abingdon Press, 1969.

CHAPTER 6

Bright, John. *The Authority of the Old Testament.* Grand Rapids, Michigan: Baker Book House, 1975.

Bruce, F. F. *Tradition: Old and New.* Grand Rapids, Michigan: Zondervan Publishing House, 1971.

Bruce, F. F. *The New Testament Documents: Are They Reliable?* Downers Grove, Illinois: Inter-Varsity Press, 1943. Revised edition, 1960.

Henry, Carl F. H., ed. *Revelation and the Bible.* Grand Rapids, Michigan: Baker Book House, 1967.

Krentz, Edgar. *The Historical-Critical Method.* Philadelphia: Fortress Press, 1975.

Ladd, George Eldon. *The New Testament and Criticism*. Grand Rapids, Michigan: Wm. B. Eerdmans, 1966.

Lindsell, Harold. *The Battle for the Bible*. Grand Rapids, Michigan: Zondervan Publishing House, 1976.

Newport, John P., and Cannon, William. *Why Christians Fight Over the Bible*. Nashville: Thomas Nelson, Inc., 1974.

Packer, J. I. *Fundamentalism and the Word of God*. Downers Grove, Illinois: Inter-Varsity Press, 1958.

Perrin, Norman. *Rediscovering the Teaching of Jesus*. New York: Harper and Row Publishers, Inc., 1976.

Ramm, Bernard. *The Pattern of Authority*. Grand Rapids, Michigan: Wm. B. Eerdmans, 1957.

CHAPTER 7

Barclay, William. *Ethics in a Permissive Society*. New York: Harper and Row Publishers, Inc., 1972.

Bell, Daniel. *The Cultural Contradictions of Capitalism*. New York: Basic Books, 1976.

Brown, Harold O. J. *Christianity and the Class Struggle*. Grand Rapids, Michigan: Zondervan Publishing House, 1971.

D'Aprix, Roger M. *Struggle for Identity*. New York: Dow Jones-Irwin, Inc., 1972.

Emerson, William A., Jr. *Sin and the New American Conscience*. New York: Harper and Row Publishers, Inc., 1974.

Fletcher, Joseph. *Situation Ethics: the New Morality*. Philadelphia: Westminster Press, 1966.

Fuller, Reginald H., and Rice, Brian K. *Christianity and the Affluent Society*. Grand Rapids, Michigan: Wm. B. Eerdmans, 1966.

Furness, Charles Y. *The Christian and Social Action*. Old Tappan, New Jersey: Fleming H. Revell Co., 1972.

Heilbroner, Robert L. *Business Civilization in Decline*. New York: W. W. Norton and Co., Inc., 1976.

Heilbroner, Robert L. *The Worldly Philosophers*. New York: Simon and Schuster, 1953. Revised ed. 1972.

Henry, Carl F. H. *Christian Personal Ethics*. Grand Rapids, Michigan: Wm. B. Eerdmans, 1957.

Moberg, David O. *Inasmuch: Christian Social Responsibility in the 20th Century*. Grand Rapids, Michigan: Wm. B. Eerdmans, 1965.

Niebuhr, Reinhold. *Moral Man and Immoral Society*. New York: The Scribner Library, 1932.

Rahtjen, Bruce D. *Scripture and Social Action*. Nashville: Abingdon Press, 1966.

Seifert, Harvey. *Ethical Resources for Political and Economic Decision*. Philadelphia: Westminster Press, 1972.

Silk, Leonard, and Vogel, David. *Ethics and Profits*. New York: Simon and Schuster, 1976.

Sheldon, Charles M. *In His Steps*. New York: Pyramid Publications, 1897.

Sider, Ronald J., ed. *The Chicago Declaration*. Carol Stream, Illinois: Creation House, 1974.

Sider, Ronald J. *Rich Christians in an Age of Hunger*. Downers Grove, Illinois: Inter-Varsity Press, 1977.

Simon, Paul. *The Christian Encounters a Hungry World*. St. Louis: Concordia Publishing House, 1966.

Tittle, Ernest. *Christians in an Unchristian Society*. New York: Association Press, 1939.

Vaughan, B. N. Y. *The Expectation of the Poor*. Valley Forge, Pennsylvania: Judson Press, 1972.

Weber, Max. *The Protestant Ethic and the Spirit of Capitalism*. New York: The Scribner Library, 1938.

CHAPTER 8

Baldwin, James. *Another Country*. New York: Dell Publishing Co., 1960.

Baldwin, James. *The Fire Next Time*. New York: Dell Publishing Co., 1970.

Baldwin, James. *Nobody Knows My Name*. New York: Dell Publishing Co., 1961.

Campbell, Ernest T. *Christian Manifesto*. New York: Harper and Row Publishers, Inc., 1970.

Campbell, Will D., and Holloway, James Y. *The Failure and the Hope*. Grand Rapids, Michigan: Wm. B. Eerdmans, 1972.

Clark, Kenneth B. *Dark Ghetto*. New York: Harper and Row Publishers, Inc., 1965.

Cone, James H. *God of the Oppressed*. New York: Seabury Press, 1975.

Greeley, Andrew M. *Why Can't They Be Like Us?* New York: E. P. Dutton and Co., Inc., 1971.

Grier, William H., and Cobbs, Price M. *Black Rage*. New York: Bantam Books, Inc., 1969.

Halseden, Kyle,. *The Racial Problem in Perspective*. New York: Harper and Row Publishers, Inc., 1939.

Hamilton, Charles V. *Black Preacher in America*. New York: William Morrow and Co., 1972.

Howe, Louise Kapp, ed. *The White Majority*. New York: Random House, 1970.

Jones, Howard O. *For This Time*. Chicago: Moody Press, 1966.

Jones, Howard O. *Shall We Overcome?* Old Tappan, New Jersey: Fleming H. Revell Co., 1966.

King, Martin Luther, Jr. *Strength to Love*. New York: Harper and Row Publishers, Inc., 1963.

King, Martin Luther, Jr. *Why We Can't Wait*. New York: Harper and Row Publishers, Inc., 1964.

Morrow, E. Frederic. *Black Man in the White House*. New York: MacFadden Books, 1963.

Osofsky, Gilbert. *Harlem: The Making of a Ghetto*. New York: Harper and Row Publishers, Inc., 1966.

Pannell, William E. *My Friend, the Enemy*. Waco, Texas: Word Books, 1967.

Perkins, John. *Let Justice Roll Down*. Glendale, California: G/L Publications, Regal Books Divison, 1976.

Perkins, John. *A Quiet Revolution*. Waco, Texas: Word Books, 1976.

Rich, Andrea L. *Interracial Communication*. New York: Harper and Row Publishers, Inc., 1974.

Salley, Columbus, and Behm, Ronald. *Your God Is Too White*. Downers Grove, Illinois: Inter-Varsity Press, 1970.

Segal, Ronald. *The Race War*. New York: Bantam Books, Inc., 1967.

Skinner, Tom. *Black and Free*. Grand Rapids, Michigan: Zondervan Publishing House, 1968.

Skinner, Tom. *Words of Revolution*. Grand Rapids, Michigan: Zondervan Publishing House, 1970.

Smith, H. Shelton. *In His Image, But: Racism in Southern Religion*. Durham, North Carolina: Duke University Press, 1972.

Thurman, Howard. *Jesus and the Disinherited*. Nashville: Abingdon-Cokesbury, 1970.

Thurman, Howard. *The Luminous Darkness*. New York: Harper and Row Publishers, Inc., 1965.

Tilson, Everett. *Segregation and the Bible*. Nashville: Abingdon Press, n.d.

Tucker, Sterling. *For Blacks Only*. Grand Rapids, Michigan: Wm. B. Eerdmans, 1971.

Wilmore, Gayraud S. *Black Religion and Black Radicalism*. New York: Doubleday/Anchor Press, 1973.

Young, Whitney M., Jr. *Beyond Racism: Building an Open Society*. New York: McGraw-Hill Book Co., 1969.

"Report of the National Advisory Commission on Civil Disorders." New York: New York Times Co., 1968.

CHAPTER 10

Anderson, Gerald, ed. *The Theology of the Christian Mission*. Nashville: Abingdon Press, 1969.

Beaver, Pierce R. *The Missionary Between the Times*. New York: Doubleday and Co., Inc., 1968.

Beyerhaus, Peter. *Missions: Which Way?* Grand Rapids, Michigan: Zondervan Publishing House, 1971.

Clark, Dennis E. *The Third World and Mission*. Waco, Texas: Word Books, 1971.

Comara, Helder. *The Church and Colonialism*. Denville, New Jersey: Dimension Books, Inc., 1969.

Costas, Orlando E. *The Church and Its Mission: A Shattering Critique from the Third World*. Wheaton, Illinois: Tyndale House Publishers, 1974.

Dodge, Ralph E. *The Unpopular Missionary*. Old Tappan, New Jersey: Fleming H. Revell Co., n.d.

Fenton, Horace L., Jr. *Myths About Missions*. Downers Grove, Illinois: Inter-Varsity Press, 1973.

Fife, Eric S., and Glasser, Arthur Γ. *Missions in Crisis*. Downers Grove, Illinois: Inter-Varsity Press, 1961.

Gerber, Virgil, ed. *Missions in Creative Tension*. South Pasadena, California: William Carey Library, 1971.

Higdon, E. K. *New Missionaries for New Days*. St. Louis: Bethany Press, 1956.

Horner, Norman A., ed. *Protestant Cross Currents in Mission*. Nashville: Abingdon Press, 1968.

James, Tracey K., Jr. *Our Mission Today*. New York: World Outlook Press, 1963.

Kane, Herbert J. *Winds of Change in the Christian Mission.* Chicago: Moody Press, 1973.

Lamott, Willis. *Church Revolution in Missions.* New York: MacMillan Publishing Co., 1955.

McGavran, Donald A., ed. *Crucial Issues in Missions Tomorrow.* Chicago: Moody Press, 1972.

McGavran, Donald A. *Understanding Church Growth.* Grand Rapids, Michigan: Wm. B. Eerdmans, 1970.

Scherer, James A. *Missionary Go Home.* New York: Prentice-Hall, Inc., 1964.

Soltau, Stanley. *Missions at the Crossroads.* Grand Rapids, Michigan: Baker Book House, 1955.

Wagner, Peter C., ed. *Church/Mission Tensions Today.* Chicago: Moody Press, 1972.

Wakatama, Pius. *Independence for the Third World Church: An African's Perspective on Missionary Work.* Downers Grove, Illinois: Inter-Varsity Press, 1976.

DATE DUE